SURVIVAL

SURVIVAL

A PREPPER'S GUIDE TO LIFE AFTER THE CRASH

STEVE MATTOON

CAMILLUS

Skyhorse Publishing

Skyhorse Publishing books may be purchased in bulk at special discounts for sales promotion, corporate gifts, fund-raising, or educational purposes. Special editions can also be created to specifications. For details, contact the Special Sales Department, Skyhorse Publishing, 307 West 36th Street, 11th Floor, New York, NY 10018 or info@skyhorsepublishing.com.

Skyhorse® and Skyhorse Publishing® are registered trademarks of Skyhorse Publishing, Inc.®, a Delaware corporation.

Visit our website at www.skyhorsepublishing.com.

10 9 8 7 6 5 4 3 2 1

Library of Congress Cataloging-in-Publication Data is available on file.

Cover design by Tom Lau

Print ISBN: 978-1-5107-0784-9
Ebook ISBN: 978-1-5107-0786-3

Printed in China

Table of Contents

Introduction

Surviving While Surviving

The signs are not good for America! There is an eighteen trillion dollar debt and growing, the possibility of a national power grid failure is a real concern and tied to the power grid is the chance of an international terrorist attack and solar flares from the sun, Ebola has become a major concern worldwide and proves a pandemic can quickly become a reality, and the list goes on.

The list goes on, but whatever national disaster befalls the country is really irrelevant. If food supplies or the distribution of life saving supplies are cut off, it does not matter what is the cause. There are studies that say if the national power grid fails for an extended amount of time, 90 percent of the country's population may perish.

There are many reasons that these conclusions are a possibility. Let's look at some facts, many of which are backed up by studies of past man-made and natural disasters. During several major hurricanes (Katrina, Andrew, Sandy, etc.), as well as many other similar events worldwide, some startling facts were determined:

- One-third of the population are day shoppers with very little emergency supplies, if any, to sustain them.

- Looting and home invasions will take place, many by armed gangs looking for food and anything to sustain them. In some past situations looting started while the event was still in progress.

- Police and emergency services will be disrupted, slow to respond, or nonexistent in certain areas.

- Individuals and groups within the populace may find themselves in a life or death survival or personal defense situation at any time, very often without warning.

With the above four things in mind, ask yourself if you are ready for long-term, or even short-term, personal or family survival, and are you prepared to defend yourself from injury or lethal threat? If the answer is yes, then you are probably a prepper, survivalist, ex-military, or outdoorsman or -woman who has thought this out and prepared. I have no official figures, but this may encompass 10 percent or so of the population. This book is for the other 90 percent, or at least those of that population who are concerned and interested. A certain percentage will say nothing is going to happen, and I hope they are correct. A certain percentage will be incapable of preparation; these are the disabled, both physically and mentally, among us. If a long-term disaster should occur, whatever you have at your disposal is what you are going to have to sustain yourself, your family, and the people you choose to help you through this dangerous and life-changing situation.

Any long-term survivalist or prepper will tell you they probably have been at it for a long time and it is an ongoing way of life. They will also tell you the reason it is a way of life is that no one knows when it will happen. Disaster has no schedule; it strikes everyone equally and without warning. Those not prepared for the long term will probably die of starvation, sickness, or as a victim of violence. There are many good survival books out there, and all have good advice. This one will be no different other than it will advise the family or group on how to Survive While Surviving. The data on basic survival is at your fingertips.

Why do I say group? Groups are harder to feed than individuals, but individuals in areas where violence is taking place are the first to die. The reasons are simple: you cannot watch all approaches to your survival location, and you cannot stay awake and functional long. Should disaster strike, everyone will be thrown into the same situation where food, water, fire, shelter, and medical care will be the five primary concerns in their lives for as long as the situation lasts. The recommendations made in this book are not guarantees. Should long-term disaster strike, the survivors will have several things in common: preparation, luck, a good survival mind-set, a good support group, and a propensity for violence and personal survival. Hopefully, disaster will not strike, but if it does, it will probably be instant with no warning. What preparation or abilities you have will be all you have to survive the event. This is a different survival manual, which explains what has to take place while you are doing everything the other survival manuals teach you. While you will have to store food properly, purify water, and all the other associated subjects in the survival field, if disaster strikes long term, you are going to need other thoughts, knowledge, and mind-set. That's what this book is about. If you think things are not going to get really rough when more than three hundred million people get their food and critical supplies cut off, no book ever written will help you including this one.

I will state it again in the following chapters, but in a long-term survival situation if society should collapse, Surviving While Surviving will be as critical as the ability to find food and water. This is the bottom line that survival books do not cover—or I have not found them. Surviving While Surviving may be initially confusing to the unprepared, who are only worried about having enough food and water. Let me throw up a couple of bullet points to get you on board and thinking. Violence is taking place and people are dying, scared, hungry, and committing violence on other people for what they have.

Some Questions to Wake You Up

- You are searching for food and water in an abandoned grocery store—who is on guard?
- You are asleep—who is on guard?
- You are cutting firewood—who is on guard?
- You have food and are eating—who is on guard?
- You are doing something that requires your full attention—who is on guard?

Hopefully you get my point. In situations like what we will be discussing in this book, if you do not have someone on guard 24/7, you and what you have to survive with will not be around long.

This book is designed to make you use your head. It has chapters that will tell you all you have to think about to survive and, most importantly, how to Survive While Surviving. Get used to this term. It will present you with more requirements for study and training than you will think possible. You will read about what you need to survive and what you need to do to Survive While Surviving. I am going to go out on a limb and estimate that 90 percent of the people who read this book will not make the effort required to prepare. The ones who do make the effort will, in the end, know that all the equipment they have acquired to survive the event is useless to anyone unless they have the mental fortitude and toughness to live, survive, and protect themselves while surviving.

When disaster strikes and people come to kill you for what you have, will you be able to stop them? Will you have the will to win? Will you have developed the mind-set to fight while you are hurt, bleeding, and having trouble catching your breath? I have friends who are preppers who are doing good things preparing for hard times, but when I question what they are preparing for, I get answers such as, "When it all ends." Personally, I am not sure what that means. I do not believe the country will fall apart tomorrow, but know that sooner or later disaster will strike in some form or another.

Who is on guard while you search an abandoned grocery store?
(wwing, courtesy of iStock)

Being prepared to fend for yourself just makes sense. On my part, that forethought comes from my time in the army. Nevertheless, the more time you spend preparing for disaster, the better you will do. I have friends with no military experience who have plans to button down and take on all comers. For those who have never been in a serious gunfight at close range, you need to realize there are usually casualties on both sides. At the least, if not hit directly with a bullet, there is a good chance you will have fragments from bullet jackets, windows, or cinder block pieces somewhere in you, and some of them may be serious wounds. Attrition in the group will start at the first serious clash with another armed group. I know in my heart that a lot of preppers have not fully considered this in their planning.

How can this happen in America or the world? It may start without warning. We wake up one day and find the banks are closed and credit cards are not working, the predicted financial collapse is here, and things will start to happen that no one wants. First it might be in our big cities and population areas and soon the rest of the country and maybe the world. We may find ourselves fighting for our lives to protect what we have in our homes.

If you do not have the internal confidence and personal fortitude to do the above, it makes no difference how much equipment you have acquired. Someone else is going to end up with it, and he or she will be the one that kills you because you didn't have the mental fortitude and capability to stop them. I believe this book is what you need to start the journey, but you will not develop the skills and the will to win by reading it, you are going to have to do the work. Your life and the lives of your family or group depend on it. It's easy to mental up; you have got to put in the time, sweat, and blood, get exhausted in training, and not let anything stop you from getting where you are supposed to go. I do not know how much time we have before disaster strikes—no one does. You will read many things in this book that the average citizen knows nothing about. What is recommended here for that part of the population will require hard work in acquiring materials, training, and rehearsal of any plans that are made. I would predict that even some preppers may not fully understand how dire our lives could become. There are no perfect answers in this book, but to the ones who will read, learn, and do the work required, get going. Now! The clock is ticking.

Chapter One

Survival Groups

There have been a lot of discussions on how big a group should be to ensure their survival. The size of the group will always be determined by circumstances, location, capabilities of individuals within the group, and the group's capability to adapt, sustain, and defend itself. If the group is not large enough, it will not be able to meet the survival requirements, and it will perish. The talks on group size will go on until disaster strikes. Unlike most things that are known, what we are talking about in this book has not happened in our country's history. If you take a realistic look at what may have to be done to survive after disaster, you will realize a small group is headed for eventual disaster in its own right. This does not mean a large group will survive if plagued with bad leadership, poor planning, or members not 100 percent dedicated to the group and its survival—in this respect a large group will eventually meet its demise.

Let's Look at Location–My Opinion

- Groups in rural or remote areas will do well or better than those in cities.
- Groups in large cities or population areas will do poorly unless trained and prepared.

- Groups who have a remote or rural area to go to will do well if they survive the trip.

- Groups who have prepared for the event will do the best with a little luck whether they live in a large population center or rural area, but this does not mean they will survive.

Note: Well-prepared and equipped groups have a better chance of surviving a long-term situation, but if they do not know how to Survive While Surviving, someone else will be eating their food and drinking their water. I can tell you from experience that living in a total tactical environment of unending waiting and watching for an attack is hard on trained combat troops. What thing that must be done to ensure your security in an open combat environment will be the hardest thing you do both mentally and physically? The very act of planning a gathering party to move into hostile areas is a daunting requirement.

There are as many ideas on what a group should have regarding capabilities or numbers as there are discussions on the topic. The thing about groups in most disasters is that you may end up with a group that is dictated by circumstances, not choice. Family groups are the first group in most disaster situations, and to keep it simple, we will look at a family group of mom, dad, kids, uncles, aunts, cousins, etc. If you are lucky, within this group will be ex-military, hunters, mechanics, etc. The truth of the matter is that it takes time and work to develop a good cohesive group to be proficient in the situations we will be talking about. The only advice I can give here is try to recruit people with talents you need, and in giving that advice, I must say this is not the easiest thing to do.

The family group is what it is; their ability to survive will be determined by desire, preparation, training, luck, and location. The bottom line is that if long-term disaster strikes and you have not prepared, your chance of surviving is greatly diminished. Within the family group, every physical or mentally disabled person will be a strain. If you take a look at the families in the United States with members on life support, taking medications to live, or disabilities requiring full-time care, you can plainly see where many of the predicted deaths will come from. One of the principal requirements in any survival or combat situation is the requirement to be able to move swiftly and with purpose. If burdened with wounded or disabled members, that ability is stripped from you and puts you at extreme risk in many survival or combat situations.

The family group will have the strongest bond and be willing to go to the extreme for group members. With a little luck and some in-family talents, the group may do well, but again location and preparation is everything. You may be forced to defend yourself daily if you live in a city or large population center. This will prevent or degrade your ability to find food, water, and other means of sustainment unless the group is large enough to support the needed efforts. In the large population areas, food and essentials will run out quickly, and defending what you have may quickly become a top priority. As we talk about the need for daily defense, food, water, warm clothing, and bedding, consider that if it's winter and heating your location becomes a top priority, it should not be lost on anyone that a two- to ten-person group will not do it. Two to ten people in a location that must be guarded 24/7, have water hauled in from a distance, and food hunted and processed in sub-zero weather will be hard-pressed to find and transport the cords of wood that will be required to get through the winter unless they had the full spring and summer to prepare. Once into a disaster, if you have not prepared, several things of consequence may take place.

- You are going to have to be prepared to defend your location 24/7.
- You are going to have to acquire food, water, and materials daily or biweekly.
- You may be forced out of your location by events or violence.
- You must have a daily sustenance and tactical contingency plan.
- You will have to have a daily sanitation plan.
- If forced to move, do you have the capability to move critical survival items? If not, what is the plan?

Whether your group is family or brought together by circumstances, you will have some daunting logistical requirements. If the group can maintain and hold its survival location, the logistics are fairly simple and generally boil down to acquiring food, water, and sanitation duties. The daily or biweekly acquiring of food and water may be what decides movement from your planned location—or life and death—and, depending on what is used or available for transportation, may be a complex problem. This problem will be determined by the availability of vehicles with gas, how far gathering groups must roam for food and water, and the overall tactical situation. Before we get into the how and why, we need to look at group capability and what they have available. Prior preparation here will save the day; lack of preparation may result in the demise of the group. The following is my take on acquiring enough food and water to sustain the group.

The logistics of providing food and water will be an ongoing daily effort that, as time goes by, will become more and more difficult. No matter what mode of transportation is used, the need to provide food and water for the group may force a move to a new location. But for now, let's talk logistics and how we are going to do it. Anything can be carried, regardless of weight, if vehicles are available. If vehicles are not available, the group has immediate and dire logistical problems. They just stepped back in time a few hundred years or longer, and transporting any materials may have to be accomplished on the backs of group members.

A Few Survival Facts

- The area you will have to travel will lengthen as days go by. Without vehicles, this will soon become unacceptable and a danger to group survival.

- The group will have to secure and defend its location and be prepared to tactically defend the gathering party. This means both the location and gathering party must be armed and equipped to take care of themselves. Both entities must have enough people to accomplish the required tasks.

- Depending on how big the group is, they may need many gallons of water per day. Fact: one gallon of water weighs 8.34 pounds, so twenty gallons of water weighs 166.8 pounds. Even with a cart that's a load, and we have not talked about food and any materials you may want.

- If vehicles are not available, gathering parties may be forced to travel for a day or more, which doesn't account for running into any tactical problems while out gathering. This drives the question of how many group members are at the survival location and if they can have people awake 24/7 for security.

- Is it better to gather materials as a group, or are the logistics of hiding or moving your critical items restricting this and pinning you to a fixed survival location? If pinned to a location, can it be realistically defended with the gathering party gone?

The answers to the last two bullet points have to be made by the group. I am sure during large disasters that groups have both survived and perished based on these decisions. Based on major disaster scenarios and the situation surrounding your survival location, whatever decision the group makes puts them in the hands of fate, and it is unpredictable whether they will survive or perish. Only history will note this, and in a national disaster no one may ever know.

Groups living in big cities or population areas will initially have primary problems to contend with while trying to sustain the group. Roving bands of hungry, desperate individuals will be looking for anything they can take by force for their own survival. If the group's survival location is identified, the chance of finding themselves under constant assault is 100 percent assured. Once found, the situation quickly turns to what you have to defend yourself with and how much of it.

In my view, it is a fact that guns and ammunition will be as important as food and water to ensure your survival. How to defend your survival location and gathering parties will require some tactical knowledge on defense, attack, and keeping yourself from being injured. In the end, defending your survival location will be as time-consuming and logistically challenging as acquiring food and water, and it can only be accomplished by a well-put-together group with the necessary skills and equipment. Keep in mind that if vehicles are not available, the more equipment you have, the harder it is to move.

No matter how much food and water you initially have, sooner or later you will run out at your survival location and will have to go looking for it—probably in dangerous and unknown situations. The size of the group and what it has available to defend itself will be the difference between success and failure. As stated above, there are many good survival books available, as well as good survival tips on the Internet. What most of these have in common is good advice on how to survive in remote areas. They have little to no information on surviving while protecting yourself from roving gangs or looters intent on taking what you have and maybe killing you in the process.

There are magazines that cover survival and home defense available at magazine racks in most grocery stores. They provide valid situational advice, and I recommend acquiring these and getting read up and trained. The problem with disaster is no one can predict how much time we have before it strikes. Once disaster does strike, everyone is in the same boat in that you are starting your survival career with what you have on hand or can quickly acquire. If you're ready, that's a very good thing, but if not, you will likely not survive for any length of time because the cards are stacked against you. I will not get into any discussions here on the morality or the law of what you can or cannot do to defend yourself, but if society has broken down and there is no law, the decision to live or die and what you must do is totally up to you.

Remember, we are not talking about surviving an earthquake or hurricane. That time frame will be days in most cases, and it is fairly safe to say law enforcement and emergency services will be back in place fairly quickly. However, if in the middle of those three days a group or individual comes to kill you for what they think you have, the next day and a half will mean nothing if you are not prepared to take care of yourself. You may have to deal with some looters or crazies, and most people, when in groups, are better equipped to do this. We are talking about a national emergency where society has broken down and the time frame is not weeks but is months or years.

If you think of the sick and disabled among us, the elderly, and the men and women living alone with no family or support group, the estimates of 90 percent of the population dying may be deadly accurate. Should a long-term situation, with its associated breakdown of society, take place, it will immediately put all citizens into two parallel and unending situations. The first situation will be true survival with all its associated problems. The second situation will be tactical with all the associated protocols of defense, attack, raids, tactical movement, ambush, surveillance, and unending group readiness to respond.

Keep in mind that if you live in a big city and a national disaster should take place, you or your group will be immediately facing well-armed, trained, and experienced groups with a propensity for extreme violence that we now call drug cartels and street gangs. These groups are already formed and dedicated to the groups' survival, and they will be a formidable force for any group of citizens to deal with. At an individual level it will be virtually impossible. Later chapters will provide some generally suggested lists for survival. Here, we should discuss group armament and combat survival equipment. In certain areas, especially when moving, the group will be concerned with long-range marksmen or snipers. In defending the survival location, close range fighting will be the norm.

Regardless of Size, the Group Should Have the Following Personal and Defensive Equipment

- Shotguns, both hunting and combat
- M4 or similar assault weapons with scope—not optics that need batteries
- Heavy caliber rifles, such as .308, 30/06, etc., with scope—not optics that need batteries
- .22 semiautomatic rifles for hunting rodents and defense
- Personal sidearms, such as 9mm, .40, and .45 calibers, etc.—in a perfect world the group should all have the same weapons
- At least one thousand rounds of ammunition per gun or more—in a long-term situation you will never have enough ammunition
- At least ten magazines per gun that requires them
- Binoculars
- Flashlights
- Two fixed-blade knives per group member
- Machetes
- Body armor
- Ballistic eye protection
- Helmets
- Elbow and knee pads
- Combat harnesses
- Utility belts
- Rucksacks
- Top of the line pellet guns with several cans of pellets, which are quiet for hunting small game
- Two canteens per member—more durable and needs less care than a hydro-pack

- Water purification tablets
- Four to six sets of extreme-use utility or tactical clothing
- Good boots
- Personal medical kits
- Extendable batons
- Pepper spray
- Hatchets or tomahawks
- Bows—either recurve, crossbows, or compound with extra strings and parts and at least fifty arrows

Note: I do not include night vision capability here for the reason that the majority of the population cannot afford it and certainly have more pressing items to spend their limited funds on. If you can get night vision capability, get it. It can be the difference in winning big and reducing friendly casualties in a night fight.

As any combat-trained person knows, the above list is not complete, but within our civilian community if you can start out with this minimum list you're in decent shape and probably better than most. As you survive the coming combat, you will acquire the equipment of the people you have to deal with. Never win a survival fight without taking your opponents' guns, ammunition, packs, and any other equipment they may have. Keep in mind every fight diminishes your ammunition supply. Never win a fight and leave opponents' guns and ammunition where they fell. It's called immediate combat resupply and potential barter equipment.

Never forget you are in a long-term survival and tactical situation, and both must receive full attention at all times. The list above, even though not complete, is logistical weight that you cannot carry in one load. Planning and weapons employment use is fundamental to success. Where are you going, how are you going to get there, and what equipment do you need? This planning process should be done every day for movement and survival location defense. For those of you who are scratching your head and saying it sounds like this guy is saying we are going to war, quit wondering. If disaster strikes, that's exactly what I am saying; you will be going to war. At least for the

A hatchet is just one of the personal and defensive equipment that you should have on hand in the case of a disaster. (mediaphotos, courtesy of iStock)

majority who have never been in the military, it will sound and feel like war.

Anyone in a survival situation is going to have to travel outside the survival location to secure food and water sooner or later. This will put the gathering party or individual in constant danger of being attacked and killed. Movement, planning, and the tactics used to support the move must be rehearsed and known by all. The gathering party must operate in a break contact mode; they cannot afford to get pinned down or in a long sustained fight, as they will not have the ammunition for this and will quickly deplete what they have stocked. When moving, stay spread out, and no one moves unless covered by someone else. Scan the direction of the move with binoculars, and have a rear guard watching your back. In my view, individuals in this situation are operating on borrowed time. It is only a matter of time before their luck runs out and they run into a situation that will get them killed. This is especially true in the big cities and high-population areas. If you have to fight, do it at a time and place of your choosing.

If you live in a big city, part of your preparation is to have all survival equipment in packs and ready to move as soon as you realize disaster has struck. You will also need vehicles that have gas to get out of town to a predetermined survival site or at least a safer rural site to start your survival attempts. Inner cities will become war zones that will quickly deplete your ammunition and defensive equipment. As in all combat survival situations, the best way to maintain your ammunition supply is to stay out of a fight or break contact before you get sucked into a sustained fight. There are several good tactics manuals and schools that teach these tactics, and since we do not know when disaster will strike, getting some training and range work that will enhance your capabilities would be in your best interest. I will discuss some basic tactics in a following chapter.

As time goes by and food and water become harder to get, the group members will weaken physically. They will not be able to stay as sharp and focused without sustenance, so a move to a new location may be in the group's best interest. As hunger sets in, anything that can be eaten will be, which includes cats, dogs, birds, rats, worms, etc. All humans have a survival gene within and will sooner or later eat what they would never have considered in good times. I am sure people reading this book will be looking for good news should disaster on a national scale strike, but I believe there will not be any.

Discipline must be enforced whether the group is a family or one put together out of necessity by known associates. Group members who become disillusioned, mentally unstable, or in constant disagreement with group decisions are a danger to the group and should be dealt with quickly. A group that is not totally cohesive and unified will perish. If discipline is not enforced, infighting will eventually break out, and the group will be degraded to ineffectiveness. Hard decisions, especially within family groups, will have to be made. Remember the grass always looks greener somewhere else when you are disillusioned, but in a national or world disaster you will be moving from one wasteland to another and there will be no green grass or a better situation. You may find and be accepted by a different group, but your day-to-day dangers and survival requirements will remain the same.

In a functional group within a survival environment, the more democratic the group is the better. Keep in mind that in survival and tactical situations, decisions have to be made quickly on a regular basis by the leaders. Everyone in the group needs to understand this, and this should be part of your preparation process. It should also be understood that in most survival and critical tactical situations, no one will have extra time on their hands. Groups should put the most qualified people in charge—not necessarily the best liked. Many protocols must be in place to ensure group survival, and here is where the size of the group is important. Whether food and water are scarce or plentiful, no one can stay awake and alert for days at a time, but things are going to have to take place 24/7. With this in mind, scheduling who does what and when are critical. Who is on guard at the survival location, who is with the gathering party, who is on guard days, who is on nights, who sleeps and when? Failure to enforce discipline and adherence to the required schedule will eventually be the cause of the group's fragmentation or demise at the hands of a more organized group.

All of the above questions are critical to the group's survival and are important to ensure the group is not surprised in their survival location or when out gathering. Having been in tactical situations for most of my life, I can say confidently that no matter how sharp or how good you are, everyone must be doing their job. Situations will arise that you have not planned for, and some will be a complete surprise and require quick and decisive action to survive. Be prepared at all times for disaster to strike the group. For example, the gathering party is ambushed and does not return. This will immediately put the group into disarray and force them to operate in a greatly diminished capacity. If not handled properly, casualties and attrition among group members will render the group ineffective. There will always be chances to increase group numbers, but be careful whom you pick, and watch them carefully until they are a proven asset. The chance you made a bad choice is as good a possibility as not.

Gathering parties will be moving constantly and most likely through constant danger areas. Their movement must be well planned and tactical—no one moves unless covered by someone else. Here is where the poorly trained or untrained get into trouble because they are generally moving beyond their weapons' capabilities to cover the moving group. To the military or police veteran this is well known, but to untrained individuals or novices thrown into the situations we are talking about, this is mostly unknown or confusing. I personally know Army, Navy, and police special operators who can regularly hit with a combat pistol at one hundred yards. If you are a person who has not spent a career on the range perfecting your skills, the following ranges should be your plan for supporting moving group members.

- Pistols: 25 yards
- Shotguns: 00 buck at 25 yards or slugs at 100 yards
- M4/M16: 600 yards with training, otherwise 300 yards
- .308/7.62: 1000 yards with training, otherwise 600 yards
- Hunting rifles: Whatever you are good at—at the farthest range you can hit a deer, you can also hit a person
- Bows: Determined by practice

Now, I know all kinds of shooters and commandos will say they can shoot said weapons farther. I agree, I have done it for more than fifty years, but I have also been on the range with civilians and will stick to the ranges stated. No one is going to have ammunition to waste. Unless it is all you have, you should not be using a pistol to support someone moving unless inside a small building. Pistols are for your close-range personal protection and everyone should have one. Are you going to find yourself in unplanned situations with the terrain or topography going against you? Count on it, plan and prepare every move, and be prepared for the worst-case scenario. Of course, this is easy for me to say, and easier said than done.

As I stated earlier, this book is not how to get survival food and water if disaster strikes. There are hundreds of books, videos, and Internet postings on the subject, so you can easily get them and train-ing. This book is how to Survive While Surviving in a worst-case scenario. In my view, if you're out gathering or processing your urine to drink and someone kills you because you're not using good tactics or security protocols, what you know about basic survival becomes a moot point. The group that is controlling its space and the space around them has a good chance of Surviving While Surviving.

We talked about guns, but what about ammunition? Fact: You will never have enough if you have to use it on a daily or regular basis. Never put someone down while defending yourself without taking his or her gun and ammunition, and anything else they are carrying is probably useful. In the past, I have generally said that for every gun you have, stock at least a thousand rounds. That's good advice for any problem that may arise, but with what we're talking about, many thousands would be better. As always, it comes down to what you can afford, when you started stocking up, and where you have to store and secure it. The bottom line is that if you have a pistol, shotgun, and assault rifle with a thousand rounds each, how are you going to move it without a vehicle? How are you going to secure it if you have to leave it for any length of time? Many people in our population do not even own a vehicle and depend on public transportation. Vehicles will be easy to get if disaster strikes, but will fuel be available and will streets be passable if days of rioting occur?

No matter what your initial thoughts are regarding what it will take to survive in a long-term situation, it will probably boil down to what you have heard or read. In a survival situation of any length of time, you will need a gun or guns to take care of yourself and the group. I would suggest you go back and read my weapon and equipment suggestions again. As time goes by and things get more critical, the group is going to be in a combat situation whether they want it or not. The group cannot only have a guard shotgun and a gathering party rifle. As in all combat situations, everyone in the group will need guns. The group needs a good mix of the guns that I recommended, and everyone needs a pistol. Do not kid yourself, things will go to hell quickly, and looters will be out instantaneously. You only have to look at what happened during Katrina or the Rodney King riots. Your group protection protocols and weapons use will be the difference in any chance of long-term survival. I am not going to preach to civilians who are set in their ways, and I do not need to preach to the ones who are preparing and on board with how to handle diverse or dangerous situations. I will say there are certain things normal people and good everyday citizens need to know to have any chance of surviving. During a long-term disaster when you have to fend for yourself, there are several things that will make your chances of survival better than most.

- **Physical Fitness**—The better shape you are in, the better you will think and be able to handle what comes at you.

- **Adaptability**—Things are not going to be the way they were, and they are going to be constantly changing. The better you are at quickly adapting, the better your chances of surviving.

- **Mental Stability**—Think, stay calm, know where you are going, how you are going to get there, and what equipment you need to make it happen.

- **Weapons Proficiency**—This includes all children old enough to make a decision and all other family members who are physically able regardless of age.

Long-term survival is a pressure cooker lifestyle, and if you do not have the above attributes, get some people in the group that do. You will find this is easier said than done. It does not matter whether the survival group is a family group or a group thrown together by the situation, there are several protocols that must be strictly enforced for the group to maintain itself and be successful. One of these is strong leadership. Having group members with military or police experience is a must in my eyes, but these members may not be good leaders. The selection of leaders and replacing leaders who are not good leaders must be a group decision and strongpoint. Only time and group organization will determine the group's effectiveness. Group organization should focus on the protocols that have worked in the past with groups in dire circumstances.

Successful Group Protocols

- There should be group rules, and they should be strictly enforced.

- Group hygiene must be a daily event and enforced by leaders.

- The group splits all assets equally between members.

- Group decisions should be voted on, including leadership positions and rules.

- Discipline must be strictly enforced.

- When moving outside the survival location, the move must be planned and tactical.

- Defense of the survival location must be planned and tactical.

- Group members who become detrimental to the group must be dealt with immediately.

- The group should understand that leaders will make the final decisions.

It would serve any group best if the above points could be laid out, agreed upon, and incorporated into group training and preparation prior to any disaster. The reality is that most groups thrown together by circumstances will have to work them out the hard way and hopefully will survive what will be a difficult and life-changing event. I am sure people reading this book will ask, "Why didn't he tell us what we need to do?" I say, go back and read the nine bullet points just listed and start getting your group and plan for survival together, as no one knows when disaster will strike. I gave you my take on where you need to go, and you have to get yourself there and make your own decisions as quickly as you can. There are people who are knowledgeable on survival that say everyone in the group should not know everything about what is going on within the group. I disagree with this because if you can't trust them while preparing, you are in trouble as a group once disaster strikes.

I do not have all the answers, and among my military buddies there are different outlooks on how to do things—they all have merit, but these are mine. For what it's worth, should disaster strike, I am following the advice in this book. Based on my fifty-plus-year career, I believe it will work, and I am willing to stake my life on it in the event of disaster. Serving in the type of units I have been in during my career has provided me with vast experience. However, that does not guarantee I will survive in a long-term disaster situation—luck or fate may go against me at the wrong time. That notwithstanding, the time I have spent in combat units and situations does guarantee that I can take care of myself and get things organized and functioning while doing it. Again, that does not guarantee success, but it raises my chances of success greatly. As stated previously, there are no perfect answers and certainly no guarantees.

Groups or individuals that live or are trapped by events in large population centers or large cities will have to go on full alert to protect what they have from looters very shortly after the event. Groups living in rural areas will have an easier time initially but should stay aware of their surroundings and not take anything for granted. There has been much written about wealthy people and their rural retreats, as well as TV programs about preppers and their stock of supplies and retreats. Among the populace, there will be groups or individuals who will look to these potential sites as salvation for a time and may be conducting recon operations on these sites already.

No matter where you are when disaster strikes, going on guard and securing yourself should be a first priority to ensure your survival efforts are successful. In the following chapters, we will discuss the differences between urban and rural settings and the more successful security measures that can be used when you are completely on your own. No book or training class can cover all that needs to be accomplished and how to accomplish it. This information in this book will stick with the basics, and hopefully if a national disaster happens, it is enough to get people who now know nothing about Surviving While Surviving to have a good start in developing what will be a must-have program for them to have any chance of surviving. This book guarantees nothing other than giving you a good start; it does not and cannot guarantee you success—only luck and how you prepare and conduct your group activities will determine this. As in all combat or high-risk situations, your first mistake may very well be your last, and this holds true for groups, as well as individuals.

Do not think that because you are in a rural or remote setting that you will not have similar problems to people who live in high-population areas. You should not have them as often or early on, but you will have them. The rural or remote site, even though removed from the most dangerous areas, still presents its own problems for the group using it as a survival site. These problems are enhanced if the area is heavily wooded or mountainous. It will be easy for a group to develop a false sense of security when in a remote area. All you have to do is walk outside at night and look up at the sky full of stars and listen. You generally hear nothing, maybe a night bird or coyote, but there is usually total silence. It is not hard to convince yourself you are alone in the world. People who have these sites, especially if they have been there an extended length of time, should suspect that other people know of their existence. If you take the percentage of the population who get out of town and head for the hills, many of these people being hunters and woodsmen, your remote site may not be remote long.

Everyday Operations That May Give Away the Location of Your Site

- Smoke from cooking or warming fires can sometimes be seen or smelled for miles.
- Noise from site maintenance will carry long distances.
- Talking or yelling will carry long distances.
- Gathering or water parties moving about may be seen by anyone in the area.

Caution! Smoke from cooking or warming fires can sometimes be seen or smelled for miles. (Dale C. Spartas/http://www.spartasphoto.com)

- People traveling through the area finding a garden or wood-gathering area will be alerted to the possibility of the site location.

- Any dump sites, old or new latrines, or fresh trails will notify anyone to your possible presence.

- Gunshots fired while hunting will attract people from miles away.

This list is not complete but hopefully gives you an understanding that you can be found at any time, whether by accident or by your actions make no difference, and once found, you will most likely have problems. Heavily wooded or mountainous terrain, although good for hiding, also presents the group with problems once their site is discovered.

Problems with Wooded and Mountainous Terrain

- The site can be observed without the group detecting the observers.

- The site can be approached without detection unless daily guards and patrols are being used.

- An attack can come quickly from close range.

- Gathering or water parties can be ambushed easily.
- The site can be broken into if the entire group leaves.

These points will hopefully drive home the point that even though you are in a remote area, your day-to-day security must be the same as any well-prepared group in a city or high-population area. In remote areas, it is easy to develop a false sense of security, and this will ensure

Mountainous areas can be good for hiding, but also present problems once the site is discovered. (Dale C. Spartas/http://www.spartasphoto.com)

that eventually your luck will run out. Group leaders and members should enforce daily security in pre-event preparations, as well as 24/7 after disaster strikes and they are in their remote location. Group leaders must keep on top of their game as far as group security goes.

As stated, it will be easy for group members in a remote location to convince themselves that they are safe and will remain that way, but nothing is further from the truth. The only good thing about a remote location is that it is hopefully hidden so looters and roving gangs will not be looking at, and possibly entering, the site daily. In cities, everyone will start looking for food and materials, and the survival site will be under siege constantly. The last thing I want to cover is the group's use and care of its weapons and ammunition management. Group leaders must check individual weapons on a regular basis, weapons should be maintained on a scheduled basis, cleaning materials should be part of the group's equipment, and ammunition should be kept clean and serviceable. Keep a loaded weapon ready when cleaning other weapons. Have weapon repair materials on hand—part of your planning should encompass weapon repair or parts replacement.

The group should be proficient in reloading and have the appropriate reloading materials on hand. These materials add weight to the group's mandatory supplies and will be problematic if vehicles are not available and a move to a new location is forced upon the group, but they are worth having. Friends from the military and law enforcement who have read this part of the book agree that my recommendations on weapons are dead on, but some people will say I am exaggerating about what weapons and ammunition should be available. Those people have not seen the myriad of dead I have seen in countries where people with weapons came to kill people who didn't have them. There is a lot of information to be thought about and trained on in this chapter, but the military-experienced will know this material and be on top of it. For the untrained, however, read carefully and do what you think you must do to prepare.

Security for your preparations must be strictly enforced because the more people who are aware of your operations outside the group, the more chance you have of being burglarized for what you are gathering. You will probably be first on the looters' list if word gets out about what you and the group are doing. The more equipment you acquire, the harder it is going to be to keep it hidden. There are several options to maintain group security.

Group Security Options

- Rotate group meetings at different group members' houses.
- Store equipment in attics, cellars, or rooms without windows.
- Rent a storage facility for storing equipment.
- The group can rent a small warehouse for trucks and storing equipment.
- If a group member lives in a secure location and has the storage facilities, do all group activities there.

The above options all have merit. Each group will have different options available and should operate accordingly. Security of the group's preparations should be the top priority for all members.

Pay attention to my next point—your life depends on it!

Never bring a knife to a gunfight, but never, ever bring nothing to a gunfight!

Keep in mind that the more time available for planning and preparation, the better will be your chance of success. Groups must stay realistic in their approach to preparation and the expected results of that preparation. Group inventories of equipment and stores must be made regularly. Acquiring equipment without the ability to move it is discussed throughout this book and should never be overlooked. Disaster potential should always be assessed. If you are storing your equipment in a structure that could be set on fire, what is the option? Most times there will not be one, and you are rolling the dice and hoping your structure is not accidentally or purposely set on fire. The further assessment is if you lose most or all of your equipment in the disaster, what are your options and where do you go?

Chapter Two

The Urban Survival Location

Within our large cities and urban areas of high populations, there are many tens of thousands of structures, neighborhoods, and business districts with high-rises and sprawling industrial areas. Within this infrastructure, tens of millions of people are living, and many of them are totally unprepared for a disaster of any kind, much less a catastrophic long-term event with its associated breakdown of life-sustaining services and society. Within the cities around the country are uncountable one-room apartments that are living space for millions of people. We will begin this chapter with the smallest living spaces occupied by people. My intent here is to initially list the pros and cons of these structures. Many are in multistory buildings with a front door, a back entrance or fire escapes, and one or more stairs to the upper floors. Some of these buildings have few windows other than on the front and back side and are either wood or brick.

Pros

- They are easily defended by a small group.
- With few accesses into the building, the chance of being surprised is limited.
- Residents can quickly form a group and share survival supplies.

Cons

- It is easy to be trapped inside by a small group.
- The few accesses into the structure are danger areas subject to ambush when leaving.
- Many citizens who live in these structures are day shoppers who do not have a large amount of food on hand.
- If the water is cut off, residents will be forced to leave the structure quickly.
- Human waste and garbage will become an immediate problem.

This pro and con list is not complete since I have to be careful to not write a book so big and heavy no one could lift it. I will try to describe some of the additional problems associated with these structures. If the structure is wood, it can easily be burned down. The good news is that looters usually loot first then burn down, although arson for arson's sake should not be ruled out. The thought of being burned out should be motivation to move early on to a safer site. Some of these structures are in old hotels with opposing or off-set rooms on each side of a hallway, but others have two or four apartments at the top of each staircase. These structures, whether wood or brick, can be easily defended, as any structure can be fortified and protected by a group. However, after reading the first chapter, the question should be how much work will it take to fortify it correctly, and is the effort worth it.

I suspect many of the people living in these structures will remain unprepared and, when disaster strikes, will become roving bands of looters out of sheer necessity. If anyone is looking for the politically correct way to say something, they will not find it in this book. If the situation we are talking about should happen, the first two things to go, as they always do in these situations, is political correctness and humanity—somewhere between those two virtues, most egos take a hike, as well. To readers of this book who cannot get on board with preparing for the most life-changing event imaginable and stick to their politically correct view, I suggest learning verbal judo. If assaulted by a roving gang of looters, maybe it will work, and I wish you luck. Personally, I will stick to the list of suggested weapons in this chapter, along with dedicated preparation and group organization.

Another drawback of wooden structures is that they have drywall construction, and any bullets fired will generally go through the entire structure. There is little to no cover, and even if you have a narrow hallway that no one can force because you have it covered, you can still be hit by return fire coming through the wall or door. Cinder block walls are a little better cover in that most pistol rounds will be ineffective when impacting them. Heavy caliber rifle rounds, on the other hand, will zip right through the cinder block unless the voids are filled with concrete. Another detriment to interior drywall construction is looters, or people who don't have your best interests at heart, will not have to force the hallway you are covering or even expose themselves to your fire. With as little effort as a few kicks, they can go through the wall and move room to room—they only have to gain access to the room at the end of the hall. This technique is not a secret; burglars and looters have done it in almost every disaster or civil unrest situation that has ever happened.

Even with cinder blocks, if looters have sledgehammers or similar equipment—and there will probably be a lot of it lying around—they can get a man-sized hole in a wall fairly quickly. It won't take much thinking to prove these types of structures are probably not where you should put your survival location. In saying that, I know if disaster strikes, millions of people will be forced by circumstances to start their survival efforts from these structures. So what can they do to prepare? Before disaster strikes it will be difficult because landlords and property owners will not entertain what has to be done to fortify the structure. We live in good times in a fairly protected society, and almost no one who is not already preparing will want to hear your concerns. As an example, if anyone had made public statements the day before 9/11 that planes were going to fly into the World Trade Center and bring the towers down, there is a good chance the authorities would have had him or her under psychiatric observation at a medical facility when the planes did hit.

So let's look at a few things we can do to harden our forced survival site in the types of structures we are now discussing. In the military, there were several instances where we had to fortify wooden structures or Quonset hut–style buildings. The military's answer to this was to bring in heavy equipment and plow up a berm of dirt around the building or fill a couple thousand sandbags and build a double or triple thick wall high enough so people standing up in said building could not be hit by direct small-arms fire. With unlimited equipment and soldiers, this was routinely done, but this is not going to happen in any town in downtown USA. Sandbags are fairly easy to come by, and you can buy bundles of them anytime you need them. With that being said, let's take a quick look at logistics.

If you live two or three floors up, you are not going to encase your building in sandbags, as it would take many thousands of bags and tons of sand or dirt. Fortifying the corners of the room would get it down to a hundred bags or so, which is still hundreds of pounds of sand and a daunting task for an upstairs dweller, but it is possible. Questions will arise from city dwellers as to where to get the sand. You may have to travel outside the city and find the right place, and you will need a vehicle and some help. If built correctly, waist-high and three deep will stop most rounds being fired through the wall and put you in command of the room. Even limiting bag numbers, this is logistically heavy and will take time. Another way would be to box the corners with several thicknesses of four-by-fours. This will be much less weight and still provide limited protection from gunfire. It's not perfect, but it's at least a little cover. Some furniture will stop pistol rounds and light rifle rounds. These are heavy couches with foldup beds, cast iron stoves, and any heavy wooden tables. Again, this is not perfect but better than nothing.

Many doors into these structures are lightweight hollow-core or particle-filled doors. These can usually be kicked in quickly for immediate entry by looters. Doors should be solid wood or metal and steel. Security doors are better but must be in reinforced jambs. Doors with burglar bars attached with a recessed slot in the floor are a good deterrent to quick entry but do not guarantee that looters or others will not get in. You must have obstacles to entry that can quickly be removed from your side in the event building evacuation becomes an immediate necessity. Any obstacles you design or build will not keep anyone out forever, but they will slow them down to where you should have no trouble hitting them with some well-aimed fire. That's how all obstacles are—they will not stop a determined effort to get in, but they will slow the intruders down so they can be engaged. All obstacles should be covered by good firing positions either inside the structure or outside. Firing positions on the outside should always be covered from inside. In a perfect world, no one should be out of sight and everyone should be covered.

Overall, the structures we are discussing are not well suited for permanent defense; there are just too many ways dedicated looters with a little experience of their own can pin you down and kill or trap you inside to where you cannot escape. I suggest anyone living in these types of structures have a planned place to go to that is more defensible and gives you a better chance of survival. This is no easy feat in the inner cities. It's going to get violent quickly once a disaster strikes on a national scale. In the early days especially, there will be no good news once panic sets in. People who have prepared and are mentally and physically able to accept reality and adapt to it will do the best. Two other problem areas in these types of structures are elevator shafts and roof access. Elevator shafts can be climbed and are an access that must be barricaded or under gun by the survival location team. If the roof can be accessed from adjoining buildings or fire escapes, you have another access to the building. The survival group that has to defend these structures safely will most likely be in a situation that requires everyone living in the building to be effective. Remember as a general rule, he who holds the high ground is in the dominant position. This is generally true in large or high-rise building defense.

As I write this, I doubt that the population that lives in these structures is adequately armed and equipped. Many are day shoppers and few have prepared for anything resembling a disaster. If you have the ability, do a tactical assessment of your survival location and the capabilities of the group. You may determine that a move to a new location is a good idea. That assessment will probably be correct, but it will also put major logistical requirements on the group in finding a new location, especially before disaster strikes, and then moving everything to it. This, again, will be easily accomplished if there are running vehicles with gas. If there are no vehicles available or roads are blocked by checkpoints or rubble, the group will have to make some hard decisions, detailed plans, and then execute and guard the move to the new location by whatever means available. There is no good advice here, as people and groups will find themselves in a myriad of situations and will have to deal with them with assets at hand.

Let's get back to survival locations. We have been talking about single- or double-room walk-ups and their associated problems as a survival location. Stepping up to wealthier apartments with multiple rooms does not necessarily mean you have a better deal. Of course you can store more food, water, and supplies, but on the other side of the equation, you still have the same and possibly larger security problems. In securing these apartments as survival locations, you still have the tactical problems of the single- or double-room walk-up.

Problems with Apartments

- Hallways
- Elevators
- Stairways
- Walls that won't stop bullets
- The need to fortify corners or dominating areas in the apartment
- Roof accesses
- Through-wall access in the case of drywall construction
- Human waste and garbage become an immediate problem

Doorways will be the first attempt by looters or raiders to access the structure. In upper-end apartments, the doors are usually stronger solid wood, metal, or steel and can easily be made into a harder entry by barricading. This never guarantees stopping anyone permanently, but it should slow them down, give early warning, and hold them outside for a period of time so gunfire can be delivered if needed to defend your survival location. Remember, for everything gained, something else may be lost. Where the single-room walk-up may require a small group to safeguard the location, the bigger and more complex the apartment or building, the more people will be needed to safeguard it, especially on the ground floor. This means more equipment, food, water, and other essentials will be needed to sustain the group, and any forced move will be more complicated or disastrous. These decisions will have to be group decisions. In the case of smaller structures and smaller groups, fatigue will be a problem, as will reacting to multiple problems.

Even though your group is in an upper-class building with more rooms and capabilities, the group is still going to have to send out gathering parties. The group will be faced with the reality of having to negotiate the same hallways, stairways, and limited exits from the building. The chance of being easily trapped in the building or ambushed while coming or going by any outside armed group of looters is very real. There will be one thing going for people trapped by other groups, and that is in a dire survival situation, the looters may not be able to hold the surrounding ground long before they have to go find food and water themselves. One thing every group should do is ration food immediately when disaster strikes. Eat the perishable stuff before it spoils, but do not try to maintain regular meals. If you do not know the extent of the disaster and how long you or the group will have to survive, start rationing immediately.

I think that even in a national emergency, some things will continue to work at least for a while. I said I am not going to waste time repeating the hundreds of redundant survival lists that are already available, but I recommend that when power is lost, everyone—group or individual—should have a solar-powered emergency radio to get any information being broadcast on conditions and future plans. There are also hand-cranked radios, which I prefer, and I suggest having two or three of these small extremely cheap lifesavers. I guarantee if you only have one, the village idiot or a four-year-old doing what they do will break it and put you out of whatever communications may be available. Those communications could be the difference between life and death or, more importantly, hope and mental well-being.

Any type of inner fortifications you build will be just as much of a logistical problem or even more than for a smaller apartment. No one here is exempt; it must be a group effort, and it will take time. I will go out on a limb here and say if you try fortifying before disaster, you are going to have issues with landlords, neighbors, police, utility personnel, and probably all of the above. It is also a given that in the event of a true national disaster, all these problems associated with doing it before will disappear and be immediately replaced by the necessity to survive. Do not forget that the reason for this book is to teach the untrained to think. While gathering materials to fortify your survival location, you will be in a dangerous environment. Gathering parties will have to maintain guard while gathering, and the survival location will have to be protected. Also keep in mind that we are talking about a true national disaster. If it's a local disaster that is going to be stabilized in a few days or so, you may lose a little sleep and have to fire your shotgun a couple times to make looters find an easier target, but in the end you will most likely be okay.

Let's move up to the individual residence in a highly populated area. There are tens of millions of these nationally of all shapes and sizes, and surrounding areas range from small city lots to several-acre pieces of property. Some of these structures are easily defendable, but some are not, either due to construction or location. In any event, the groups or families living in these structures should have a plan if they have to abandon the location due to circumstances. The plan should be the standard that you will see throughout this book of where am I going, how am I getting there, and what equipment do I need to be successful.

On private lots, no matter the size, take a look first at approaches into your survival location. Most yards in housing complexes mirror each other, were built by the same contractor, and have the same type and amount of foliage, sidewalks, driveways, street widths, and windows and doors to observe, shoot out of, egress the structure, barricade, and defend. With this being said, look out each window and determine, if things were to go as bad as we are discussing, what neighbors' houses would present a problem for you if they were occupied by someone shooting at you. Your first decision is, if you have walls that bullets can zip right through, where do you have to harden up? Where will you most likely have to shoot out of your windows or doors? A simple but expensive hardening of your house is to make the exterior double red or gray brick. This looks good, is acceptable to your neighbors or housing authority, and will stop most bullets fired at your house. Remember I said most, not all.

Once you have this plan down, the next and closer problem is foliage on the property. You do not want concealed firing positions that can engage you by surprise at a close, accurate range or approach routes that come right up to the structure's outside walls. The bottom line is if it all crashes and your group is in survival mode, those beautiful hedges and rose bushes you have been working on may need to be taken down to ground level. From a tactical standpoint and personal experience, I can tell you without reservation that people with no cover or concealment are a lot easier to hit than those who are concealed. In the long run, it saves invaluable ammunition that you are going to need later. Keep in mind that if you live in a state where winters are cold, any trees or large bushes you cut down should be cut up for winter firewood. When cutting up firewood, make sure some group members are watching the surrounding area to ensure you are not attacked by surprise.

Firewood should be stored where it can be protected and not in a place where it provides cover and a firing position for looters or groups that are on the prowl for anything that is easy to get. Once again, it is a 24/7 job of controlling your space and the space around you—always secure yourself or pay the price. Once you have cleared the area of foliage and have picked the best firing positions to defend those approaches into your survival location, the unending guard and observation of those areas becomes a full-time job. Failure to do this may result in the quick destruction of the group and the looting of the survival site.

The group should pick a survival location rally point in the event the group for whatever reason cannot successfully defend the site. If it is determined that an evacuation is required, a point should be picked that is out of sight from the survival location and maybe, depending on the density of buildings, should be several blocks away. Every group member should know where this location is and be able to get there in the dark. The group should have a group recognition code or, in military terms, a running password so members arriving in the dark can be easily identified. If things go as planned, there is still a chance some group or family members may become separated during the evacuation, especially in the dark.

As previously discussed, sandbags and timbers, such as four-by-fours, can be used for cover. If you do not have bullet-stopping walls, cut firewood of a good size stacked inside at the right locations does two things for you: it gives a little more ballistic protection and puts firewood inside, where you do not have to go outside and expose yourself to get it. The problem here is if it's cold, you are burning your enhanced ballistic protection. Group members protecting the survival location should be using binoculars and, in a perfect world, have scopes on their rifles. The survival location should have an emergency plan that sends everyone to defensive positions if the location is approached or attacked.

If you have a survival location that is on a slab, another good technique is to cut a three-by-three-foot hole in the floor of the center of each room, or where you can best cover the windows and door.

Once you have exposed the slab, you are looking at eight to ten inches of concrete. Cut a hole of the same size in the concrete. This is best done with power tools before the power goes out. Once you have exposed the dirt under the concrete, dig a chest-deep hole that you and group members who are securing other rooms can fight out of and get their heads below ground. With these positions, it does not matter if you do not have bullet-stopping walls. You will surprise anyone coming through a door or window.

Again, this is best done with the power on and using impact chisels to get through the concrete. If you own your own house and are preparing for the worst, it is a simple carpentry task to make a wooden cover for the fighting position. You can then redo your floors, and when the power goes off and things get bad, it's a simple matter of tearing up your carpet, wood, or tile floor. I know a couple of preppers who have done this, and no one knows the positions are there. Taking this step will provide you with enhanced security if your survival site is attacked. Bullet-stopping walls are still a good idea, as you will observe, as most probably shoot out of windows to defend the location.

Do not forget that windows are also an entrance into your location and need to be barricaded, especially on the ground floor. Many ground floor windows in cities have security screens or bars already on them. In brick or stone buildings, if you had to protect yourself, you have bullet-stopping walls and easily defended windows. Along with what we have already discussed to this point and will continue to talk about, you are working on hardening your urban survival site to have a chance of defending it without becoming an immediate casualty.

There will be people who say that preparation like we are discussing is over the top and paranoid. They may be right, but if you do not prepare for long-term disaster and it strikes, you may spend part of the time you have left to live telling yourself how stupid you were for not doing it. Either way it goes, if you take these steps you have given yourself and your group some enhanced survival capability. However, if you get run out of the site by extreme circumstances, someone else may benefit from your work. There are no good answers here and of course no guarantees.

Although it is a necessity to fortify your survival location, all fortifications can be penetrated. However, they will slow attackers down so they can be fired on more easily. There are a few things that can be added to the equation that come under the heading of booby traps. In the military, there are numerous devices that are made commercially for different applications. These will not be available to the general public in a survival situation, but there are a couple of easy options known to narcotics dealers and other paranoid persons that would be good in a survival situation where defense of your location and well-being is important. The first is spike boards that can be placed indoors or outdoors along suspected approach routes. They are simply made by driving nails through a wooden board and placing them in areas you want to restrict or make difficult for approach on foot. The second easy trap is hanging fish hooks at chest level in hallways, doorways, and windows. The best are treble hooks that have three prongs. Hang them with fishing line, cord, or steel wire. These will definitely slow anyone down, but the group must remember where they are so friendlies do not run into them by mistake. I do not joke here—around the world in the fight on terror the number of bad guys who have blown themselves up making bombs or running into their own booby traps is in the hundreds if not thousands over the years.

Another technique of ambushing people trying to enter your survival location is to build raised platforms above your corner positions and doorways where you can position yourself just below ceiling level. People entering structures against other armed people are seldom looking up. Their concern is rightfully looking into the room for armed defenders. The previously discussed dug-in floor positions and raised fighting positions will catch most, if not all, looters by surprise and put you in tactical control. Quick accurate fire is required here, so do your range work while you still have time.

These corner positions are easily built with lumber and a few carpentry skills. Once concealing bushes and sheds have been cleared out of the yard to expose approaches to your location and the discussed work on the structure's corners, floors, and walls have been completed, you will have a fairly hardened, easily defendable survival location. It must be understood that the site will only be as effective as the people manning it. Even with good people, if the gathering parties are not finding food and water, a forced move from your picked site may be mandatory to keep the group from becoming ineffective due to lack of sustenance. This will be a hard decision that strains the capability of the group. The act of moving critical survival equipment may be a daunting task if vehicles are not available. There are numerous things that impact the survival situation if a move from the chosen location is forced by circumstances. The biggest one is if vehicles are not available, how are you going to move what may be a ton or more of critical equipment? Dollies, garden carts, handcarts, wheelbarrows, and the like would be needed. Most group members will be pushing or pulling some type of wheeled device, but some members will be required to guard the move. The move should be intelligently planned and rehearsed using these points:

- Where are you going?
- How are you going to get there?
- What equipment do you need?

Keep in mind that just about all decisions that may have to be made in a long-term survival situation will be life or death decisions. Some may need to be made quickly, including the decision to move from the survival location, and the group may not have the capability to move everything they need. In situations like this, the stronger the group is emotionally and the closer the individual ties are within the group, the better the chance of making the right decision without fragmenting the group into infighting that will quickly destroy any chance of group or individual survival. No one can predict what situations will confront the group and what effect it will have on them. The longer a group is together and the more it prepares and trains, the better it will be when things go bad.

I think a little information on group and individual sanitation is warranted. Human waste and any garbage will quickly become a serious problem no matter the size of the survival location. Rule one should be no garbage or human waste allowed left in the structure. The military digs latrines, which are deep holes in the ground with a structure over them and seats to do your business. When they are full, lime is put over the waste, the hole is filled, and a new one is built. If the ground is too hard to dig, cut-off barrels are used under the seats and the waste is burned daily by pouring diesel fuel over it. Some hikers and backpackers dig a small hole to do their business and then cover it up. In most FEMA and short-term disasters or functions, such as sporting events or construction sites, porta-potties are used. The reason for all these is the prevention of disease. If not done correctly in the survival location, it will not matter how well you are equipped and trained once sickness sets in and decimates the group. A latrine should be dug for the survival location, and whether in a rural or remote location, it should be a minimum of one hundred feet away—and two hundred would be better. The group should monitor this, and all group members should use it. As in the old days, you will find this exciting in the winter months.

In a survival situation like we are discussing, a latrine away from the survival location due to a lack of water becomes an easy ambush position for looters who discover it. All garbage should be burned to kill germs. This helps site sanitation but will attract looters or raiders. Nothing should be left to fate; everything should be planned and rehearsed. Even with plans being rehearsed, you should be prepared for failure or if you find in the middle of the event that they are incomplete. Hopefully, rehearsal will show these deficiencies. Nothing is for sure in these situations, but the stronger the bond between group members, the better chance of success. Never prejudge how a plan is going to come out.

I have used the term looters or raiders, and I am sure people reading this will ask, "Aren't these the same?" In my mind they are two different groups.

- Looters: Will attack your location for the purpose of getting what you have and taking it back to their survival location.
- Raiders: Will attack your location with the intent of making it their own.

Let's talk about water or the lack of. If there is water, there will be no issues. If there is no quick water available, especially in the summer, all urine should be saved and put into solar stills to provide drinking water. Solar stills require a hole dug into the ground in an area that gets full, all-day sun, a sheet of plastic, a rock to weigh down the plastic, and a container to catch the purified water. They must be exposed to the sun for the majority of the day, so make sure you check on a sunny day to ensure you are putting the still in the right place. There should be a still for each group member, as stills do not provide a lot of water. There are numerous websites explaining this simple device and survival schools that teach how to fabricate it. Finding a good place to dig these in an urban area may be difficult. Some people say you can just drink your own urine in an emergency, and they are right, but this only works for a short time. When you discharge urine, it is full of waste that runs the range of calcium, potassium, sodium, some undigested alcohol, and more. The problem with these chemicals is that your kidneys got rid of them for a reason, so if you drink unpurified urine for the long term you will get sick. Medical help may be nonexistent, so that is not in your best interest.

As people read this book there will be those who say, "No way am I doing that, it will be too much trouble." I have no issues with that thought, but I strongly believe that type of thinking in the situation we are talking about will quickly be your demise. Decisions made or not made are options all humans have—whatever option anyone chooses is okay with me as long as it does not affect my personal or group survival. This chapter covers urban survival locations, but I will occasionally insert things as I think about them even though they may not have anything to do with the chapter. Most, such as sanitation, will affect all survival locations and are generally good advice.

In all cities and most high-population centers, there are a myriad of commercial and government buildings that are usually of brick or stone construction, possibly with steel or metal doors and very good security bars over the windows. At best they have bullet-stopping walls and are easier to barricade against entry. On the down side, they are large, and even when a group occupies them as a survival location, there is a possibility the building could be entered without the group knowing, and an attack could be launched on the group from close range. On the up side, these structures are usually filled with equipment or heavy-duty furniture that will allow a group to pick a good place in the building to fortify to the extreme. These large structures are generally surrounded by wide streets and parking lots, which makes defense of the site easy in some instances. These structures are also ideal for an individual or small group to hide in for a short amount of time. Long-term hiding may be possible, but if it's cold and a fire is needed or moving about for gathering food or water is a necessity, sooner or later you will attract attention from someone who does not have your best interests at heart.

If using one of these larger structures, the protocols for sanitation and group cleanliness do not change. The failure to pay proper attention to sanitation and hygiene will invariably result in disaster. There are commercial areas in all cities where the buildings are sheet steel or corrugated metal; these are not bullet-stopping walls. In these older areas, streets and alleys are narrow and empty lots are overgrown. The only reason to enter these areas would be looking for warehouses that may have something useful left in them or abandoned vehicles that may provide additional survival materials, such as gas, diesel, or oil for lubricating weapons or starting fires. They may also provide good sites for caches of needed equipment.

In dangerous survival situations, people act differently when it comes to where they feel safe from their fears or whatever is after them. Some will seek the highest floor of a multistory building, others will feel more comfortable on the ground floor, and others will seek the basement or nearest accessible sewer. I have seen this in many countries and situations where danger threatened people. Wherever you decide to go, an assessment should be made on what choices are available to you and the consequences of any given area.

Consequences of Different Locations

- If I go high: Can I be easily trapped, can I escape without going down, do I have the capability to outlast a siege, and what are my tactical options?

- If I stay at ground level: Can I be easily trapped, can I escape by going up, can I be attacked from close range, can I outlast a siege, and what are my tactical options?

- If I go low or underground: What are my tactical options, and what was I thinking? Cellars and most underground areas sooner or later become traps with no option for escape.

Remember, you are in two parallel 24/7 situations: one is survival and the other is tactical. It generally holds true that no matter what the situation, there will be good people in any urban area who may want to join the group. Group leaders will have to make decisions on whom to trust to help the group survive. Hard choices will have to be made when dealing with people, as there may be groups bartering for anything that might be trusted, there may be people who want to join a group to enhance their chances of survival, and there will be people who will try to join the group to betray it. There will be no easy or clear decisions. At the end of the day, the group's protection and survivability should be the driving force behind all decisions, and leaders and group members alike should never forget that all circumstances are tactical situations. Whatever decision is made, the group will live or die by it, as have numerous groups caught in war or survival situations throughout history.

It is hard to live that way, but it generally keeps you alive and in the game. Everything we have talked about will become harder and harder once weakness from lack of food or water sets in. Once people start becoming lethargic and have trouble focusing or staying awake, bad things are in their future. If the urban area is not providing what is needed to survive, the decision to move or leave it entirely must be made before the group becomes too weak to function. There is no guarantee that moving will be successful, but you may have a better chance of finding needed food and water. You have no chance sitting around feeling sorry for yourself while waiting to die.

When moving in an urban area—whether you are gathering, moving out of the area, or moving through it—everyone should be on alert. As stated, no one moves unless covered by someone else. Moves are planned, and even if the group is pushing handcarts or the like, moves are made from cover to cover. A rear guard should be used, and everyone should be using binoculars. The chance of an ambush from any point is a distinct possibility in any urban area. Groups cannot get into a standoff fight, as this will quickly deplete their ammunition and ability to successfully defend themselves. Prior preparation and range work that will enable you to accurately engage targets is mandatory to success. In large urban areas, you may be fired on from one of thousands of windows and not be able to identify where the fire is coming from. If so, get out of the area as quickly as possible.

This book, as well as other survival books and schools that are readily available, teaches you how to prepare for a long-term disaster, but it is your responsibility to get it done. I have been asked why I do not start a school to instruct what is in this book, and the simple answer is that I am too old and my bad attitude is getting worse. Keep in mind that no book will get the group to work well together over varied terrain and situations. You are going to have to get out and train, get your hands dirty, and sweat and bleed a little because if you only read books, survival will not be in your future. Like anything else in life you are going to have to do the work to be successful.

In heavily populated areas, there will be a lot of movement as people and groups look for food and water. If your survival location is in an area where there is a lot of activity, the group members who are on guard should be watching to warn the group of impending problems. If, for instance, you see an armed group making a tactical move on your survival site, they probably do not have your best interests in mind. However, it is possible they are just being careful, as I have previously recommended. The group needs to have contact rules for the site. The best way to determine a group's intentions is to put up warning signs and then verbally challenge their approach. If a bullet flies by your head, they are most likely not friendly.

The warning sign should say something along the lines of IF YOU PASS THIS SIGN WITHOUT VERBAL PERMISSION YOU WILL BE SHOT. Once verbal communication is made, have one of the group come forward without his or her weapons. Watch what the rest of the group does while this is taking place. Hard decisions will have to be made here. No one will ever know for sure what contact with other groups will bring until that contact is made. The group that has good security protocols and knows its area well should be successful. Never let an unknown group that is numerically superior to your group into the survival site. They stay outside, go their own way, or the fight is on.

No matter what the situation, contact with other groups or individuals will take place, and in the early days of an event it will probably be quite frequently. Keep in mind that bartering will be taking place, and there may be some semblance of organization. Neighbors may be helping neighbors, and this would be good and will enhance everyone's chance of survival. On the other hand, groups who are shooting at your survival location are definitely not your friends, and you should act accordingly. I hope that if disaster strikes, people will pull together, assist each other, and put up a united front against looters and raiders. In some areas, I am sure that will happen, but in others I am sure anarchy will reign.

In both areas, the groups and individuals who have thought this out and are prepared will do the best. No one can say what the end results will be if a national disaster strikes. Only history will record this. In an urban environment, an attack can come from any quarter. Some of the hardest fighting the military does is in cities; casualties are regular and common with ammunition expenditures being extremely high. Any attack directly on the survival location will be supported from the nearest surrounding buildings. The range to these buildings should be known, and the proper weapons must be in place to engage them in the event of attack.

The group will not have and cannot expend the ammunition that the military does. Do not shoot to feel good—wait until you have a target to hit. Ammunition management must be a group strongpoint and something leaders enforce. This is easier said than done with untrained group members, but the reality is that just because someone is firing at you, there is no requirement to waste ammunition firing back. If you are protected by bullet-stopping walls or fighting positions and are not being directly attacked by people moving on your position, let the other side shoot and waste their ammunition. Wait until you are moved on and have exposed targets to hit. Do not waste ammunition by shooting back and hitting nothing; this is ammunition you will regret not having later. Make no mistake, you must train to get people to do this. Experienced fighters do this, but most of them have years of training and combat experience.

In all urban areas, there are buildings with shelters, safe rooms, panic rooms, or barricaded spaces where people that are threatened go to hide. These work fairly well if a call can be made and the police respond to deal with the problem. In situations discussed in this book, these safe areas will become places where you are trapped. With time, and there will be plenty in a long-term disaster situation, looters or raiders who find these safe areas will have all the time they need to break into them with any tools they may acquire. If it was made by man, it can be destroyed by man. It will depend on how much time they want to take to get it done. With that being said, there are upper-end safe rooms that can only be afforded by the wealthy. These have armored and blast-proof walls and doors, are brilliantly concealed, are stocked with food and water, have bathrooms and weapons, can emit smoke and gas, have battery-powered cameras to observe outside, and would take a wrecking crew with equipment to get into.

I have talked about defending your survival site in the city or suburbs and a little about moving around in your surrounding area and the requirements to protect yourself and the group. Now let's talk about what may happen in what time frame and how it will impact everyone in the area. I have no idea what will initiate a national disaster, but with the national power grid in the news as a possible disaster, I will use that as an example.

We have some models if we look at regional power outages that happened on the East Coast in 1965 and 1977. Since we are discussing urban areas, we will use New York City as our example.

1965: In 1965, a major blackout affected the states of Connecticut, Massachusetts, New Hampshire, Rhode Island, Vermont, New York, and New Jersey, along with the province of Ontario, Canada. It struck thirty million people living in an eighty-thousand-square-mile area without warning. In New York City at the end of the night of the blackout, five cases of looting were reported. Those incidents were the only reported problems due to the blackout. The usual daily crimes reported were actually the lowest crime rates recorded since the city was keeping records. In this instance, there were no issues, emergency services continued to function and respond to calls, and people went about their business in the dark. Power was restored the next day. I believe that if the blackout had lasted longer, people would have continued to pull together and things would have been okay until critical supplies were interrupted.

1977: On July 13 at 8:37 p.m., a blackout hit the New York City power grid. Unlike in 1965, within an hour of power going out, major looting began to take place. Along with the looting came arson, and fires began to burn in several parts of the city. Emergency rooms saw the initial trickle of injuries that would turn into a flood of the injured. These early actions by looters strained the on-duty watch, and the police department put out an all-hands-on-deck call that initiated a department-wide callout.

Compounding the issues, communications were spotty, and phones were not working for the most part. Within the city, four thousand people had to be evacuated from subway tunnels. Additionally, all automobile tunnels into the city were closed due to carbon monoxide levels that could not be vented with the electricity out. LaGuardia and JFK airports were shut down. With officers responding to the all-hands call, police began making arrests, which would total more than four thousand by the end of the night. Once the arrest of looters began, serious street combat between police and looters turned the trickle of casualties in emergency rooms into a flood, which included more than five hundred police officers injured in the event. Looters also added to the count as they fought amongst themselves to steal what had already been stolen.

By the end of the night, more than sixteen hundred stores were looted with many being burned. The New York Fire Department responded to more than one thousand fires. Studies of these two events suggest that because the 1965 event started in the day when people were at work, the violence of 1977 was averted.

Without communications in an event like the 1977 blackout in New York, looting and street violence might be happening in your immediate area. You might perceive it to be a nationwide event, so you might decide to get out of town and head for your rural site

In 1977, a blackout in New York City led to major looting of stores such as the one pictured here. (AP Photo/Ed Bailey)

if you have one. In that case, you would quickly get the word that everything was over and you could go home.

Let's look at another incident in an urban area. The power went out, along with communications, during the Rodney King riots. Everyone knows what caused that incident, but I am using the statistics of that event to put your mind into thinking gear. I will not comment on the riots—just the results of what happened.

The End Result

- They lasted six days.
- 11,000+ arrests were made.
- 2,000+ were injured.
- 53 deaths resulted, 10 of those shot by police or military.
- 1,100 buildings were destroyed.
- 3,600 fires were set.
- 3,500 National Guard, Army, and Marines were deployed to assist LAPD.

All other law enforcement agencies, whether state or federal, were on the street assisting local authorities during the incident.

If the lights and communications are out and the equivalent of the Rodney King riots is taking place to make your city look like a war zone, do you make the move or not? Some people likely would. If I were leading a group, I would certainly move out of the city, but I would stop at the first secure location I could find outside the war zone to get information.

Keep in mind that in both of the described incidents of violence, the government and emergency services were working and the government was functional. Certainly, emergency vehicles would be up and down the roads, as well as other vehicles, so I would hold until I got information from somebody that said if I should go or stay.

This is a hard group decision. As previously discussed, if cities along your route are having trouble, you may have to go use an alternate route. If circumstances are really bad, you may need to start your survival right where you happen to be. Nothing is assured, so have a backup plan and a backup plan for your backup plan. If it is a true national disaster and you have information that it is, get going quickly before your movement routes are blocked. No one can predict what is going to happen—I wish I could. But even in the worst of national disasters, there will be areas of calm with people pulling together and local governments functioning. If the group can make it to one of those areas, the chance of survival will be enhanced. I base what I have said in this chapter on what I have seen in my career. The line between civilization and anarchy is thin, and you only need to read history to realize that fact has been proven over any other.

If you stay in an urban area as your survival location, I would suspect that if things turned to violence, the streets would quickly become cluttered with vehicles and wreckage. Moving through them will be difficult if you are in vehicles. Another thing, among the myriad of things that need to be planned for, is multiple flat tires from running over debris. At this point, going to a tire shop for repairs may not be possible, so add to your list of stores several spare tires for every vehicle you have. This may not be a big deal in the long run, as quickly after disaster and the disruption of services, fuel is going to be hard to get. I also will stick to my initial advice that if you are not preparing, start now. Make plans, and I recommend one of those plans being that if you live in an urban area, plan to get out.

Should disaster strike, there will be millions of people trapped by circumstances, and they will not have the ability to evacuate to a remote area. This part of the population has a good chance of dying. I believe this was considered in the study that predicted as much as 90 percent of the population will die if we lose the power grid. Sadly, there will be nothing that can be done for these people. As panic sets in and they start starving, they will become roving bands of desperate looters looking for anything to help them survive. This large group of the population is justification for arming yourself along the lines suggested in this book. Up until disaster strikes, and I hope it doesn't, there will be arguments about the suggestions in this book. After disaster strikes and the looting rampage begins, many will find out too late that they should have armed themselves, and they will stand a good chance of becoming part of the predicted 90 percent.

The intent here is not to get into a discussion on the Second Amendment or people's personal like or dislike for weapons. If disaster strikes and you are not ready to defend yourself and your family or group based on past wars and disasters, I see no reasonable way you will be around long.

Chapter Three

The Rural Survival Location

Rural survival locations make the occupants' life easier than in urban areas. The rural location is safer, but in the event of disaster on a grand scale, it is still going to be a target for looters or raiders. I have friends who have bought land in Montana, Wyoming, and other rural states so they have a place to go. Some of that land is in remote areas that have no structures on the property; others have structures already. There are basically three plans in place, and all have merit—all of these friends are former special operations types or police officers, so tactical and survival thinking was part of their plan. The initial danger for this group as stated will be the move through areas where rioting or blocked routes will interfere with well-laid plans.

Three Possible Plans

- The property has no structures on it. Structures will be built once the property is occupied. All material and equipment for survival and defense will be driven in by vehicles owned and procured for this purpose.

- There is a structure on the property that will be occupied when disaster strikes. All survival and defense material and equipment will be driven in by the owners.

- There are structures on the property that are stocked with basic gear and equipment. They are lived in by group members and maintained for the arrival of the rest of the group, who will drive in the large part of the survival and defensive equipment. These maintenance personnel are usually retired group members who are happy to be away from people and the stress of modern life.

I am sure there are other workable plans out there that have been well thought out by people with no military experience. In the first scenario, the land with no structure is used for hunting and camping vacations by the owners, which gives them the chance to learn the land and its potential. It also gives them a chance to establish contact with the locals. These contacts, if initiated and handled correctly, will pay dividends should disaster strike.

In the second scenario, the owners are not leaving any survival or defensive gear to be taken by burglars who find the structure. They can do any fortifying of the structure that they wish with no problems or distractions and can get to know the land and its potential, along with making local contacts.

The third scenario speaks for itself. Buildings can be fortified, gardens can be established, wells can be dug or water sources identified, and the property's potential can be known and used immediately once the location is fully occupied. The group members who are securing the property can make friends and contacts in the local populace. Over time, they will most likely be considered part of the local populace, which will make things easier as the situation deteriorates over time.

All of these plans depend on the owners and group members who are not on site getting there after disaster strikes. This, as stated, is the weakest part of the plan, as it depends on the extent of the damage done to the infrastructure and how fast looting gangs and raiders start blocking roads and inner arterials. Let's take a look at some potential problems that may affect these moves to the rural location. In the case of my friends who have these locations, moves of six to eight hundred miles have to be made to get there. Some have fewer than two hundred to go—in their cases the trip can be made on a single tank of fuel—but the move is still full of hazards after disaster strikes. This book is full of information meant to make you think. If disaster strikes, each area of the country will have different situations in progress. The problem for groups planning to move to a rural location will be getting information about what is going on to make an informed decision.

Potential Problems That May Impact the Move to Your Location

- No available fuel along the route—the most likely situation
- Looters or raiders blocking the route
- An EMP (electromagnetic pulse) knocks out all vehicles
- Major riots at the start location and along the route
- Raiders or looters looking for trucks to hijack for their contents
- Group members being unable to get to the start location
- Breakdown of critical vehicles during the move—always a possibility to plan for

These bullet points will give you an idea of potential problems. The list is by no means complete, many things can impact the move, but I think we have covered enough of them to open up thought processes. Let's talk about each one individually to generate discussion and assist preparation.

No Available Fuel Along the Route

This is a no-brainer; if you are going to have to refuel, you must have fuel. How far do you have to go? How many miles per gallon are you getting? That's how much fuel you need in five-gallon cans with nozzles for each vehicle to make the trip. Good sense and planning for possible route changes will have you put at least two extra tanks of gas in cans for the trip. This alone is tonnage requiring large trucks. To realistically prepare to make a group move in a survival situation with all the food, water, and needed supplies will require a large group with several transport vehicles. The bottom line is that you are going to have to move and secure tons of supplies, and the reality is that this may ultimately prove impossible to most groups. There are survivalists who say to have a seventy-two-hour bug-out bag ready to go. This is good advice, but if that's all you have, you're in trouble rather quickly after the three days.

Looters or Raiders Blocking the Route

In this instance, having communications is a necessity. If you have CB radios and a solar-powered emergency radio in each vehicle, you may get prior information on road blockages. Planning and the use of GPSs and Google Earth before disaster strikes should give you some maps of alternate routes around large cities or possible off-road routes to your location. If you are serious about planning for disaster, travel to your remote survival location by your planned routes and make sure you have enough gas on hand. Planning and running of planned routes is imperative to success. At the end of the day, based on situations in progress, you may start your survival career in an unplanned location. I am sure this happened to many pioneers when our country was being settled. There are areas in our mountain states that any route taken around towns or small cities will be an off-road route, so maps and some knowledge of land navigation is imperative. Also, in rough terrain the recovery of bogged down vehicles needs to be understood, and all vehicles should have winches.

An EMP (Electromagnetic Pulse) Knocks Out All Vehicles

Guess what, you're screwed. If all vehicles are electrically knocked out and you cannot get them going, there are few options if your rural survival location is six or seven hundred miles away or farther. You will immediately be down to few options—both good and bad. One good thing is that most, if not all, of your survival and defensive gear is where you are, so that location could become your new initial survival location by necessity. You could put as much as you can into rucksacks and handcarts and start your move to your rural location— that would be a book by itself. Then it would be your call on leaving the rest behind or burning it along with the structure it is stored in. This will be a hard decision, but if the group is intact with all your survival gear, I suggest getting to work fortifying your location to the best of your ability and taking the steps to control your immediate surroundings. It may not be an ideal situation, but things will impact all plans and may cause an immediate and drastic adjustment.

Major Riots at the Start Location and Along the Route

When disaster breaks out in your city or area that you are familiar with, get the vehicles packed—the big ones already should be—and get out of Dodge before the rioters get organized and start blocking roads with vehicles, burning tires, or whatever. Remember prior discussions in this book regarding this subject. The move will be a tactical move, and hopefully the group is big enough to have armed personnel in every vehicle. If not, drivers need to understand that they are driving the best weapon they have. The group should also try to ensure that a critical national event has happened and the move is warranted. Do not stop, and get all vehicles rolling; if you are stopped, do what you have to do to survive. I can give no further advice here without knowing what situation you get into and frankly may have no advice except do what you have to do. If you are in trouble, I suspect you will have no communication. All I can do in these circumstances is write this book and wish you good luck. Plan, prepare, and plan again.

Raiders or Looters Looking for Trucks to Hijack for Their Contents

This will take place under three conditions:

- An ambush of the trucks along a major route
- A stopping checkpoint in a constricted area along the route
- An open area stop and assault from their own vehicles

All of these instances will put the truck or trucks on the defense. All trucks should have armed group members in them to protect the driver and truck. Personal defense is going to be needed here whether from ambush, checkpoint, or attack. The reality is there may be group casualties, vehicles incapacitated, and a serious reorganization required even if you win the fight. Once spotted, any of the situations discussed are best handled by heavy, accurate firepower and quick vehicle maneuvering. If you can get off-road and bypass any potential trouble, this would certainly be in your best interests. This requires planning and training—do it or fail. I cannot give good news here; the making of a good and proper tactical move comes only from planning and training. Do not forget to take all looter or raider supplies with you if you win. Be prepared for a situation you have not planned for, as this happens frequently in combat and most survival situations.

Group Members Being Unable to Get to the Start Location

This should be expected and planned for by all groups. Plans should be made, and they will be impacted by certain critical events that may be happening. These plans should cover three basic contingencies.

- A time to be present or be left behind should be established. This should be locked in stone, and all group members should know what to do in the event they cannot make the timed assembly of the group.

- Along the route to the rural site, an assembly point should be picked where members who could not make it to the start point can be picked up by the group at a time known by all. As with the initial assembly time, this timeline should also be unforgiving. More time spent waiting will ultimately impact your ability to be successful in your move.

- The group may make an agreed upon plan to go to the missing group members' locations along their planned route to see if they need assistance and contact can be made with them. The whole group, with vehicles, would make this planned move. If disaster strikes the move, at least the group can react and hopefully not be further fragmented.

No matter what the plan, the group should decide on it together. This does not mean serious unplanned circumstances will not arise that will force an emergency change to the plan and maybe throw the group into disarray. The more you plan and the more you play devil's advocate, the better you will be able to adjust to unplanned changes. In the situations we are discussing, there is not much that will go according to plan.

Breakdown of Critical Vehicles During the Move

- Should this happen, the situation will depend on what is going on around the breakdown location. If the situation is normal and there is no threat, the drill will be to see if the vehicle can be repaired or towed. If not, can the load be redistributed to the other vehicles? If there is only one vehicle making the move and it cannot be repaired, you have some decisions to make. One is if where you are can—or should—be your initial survival location. If the answer is no, some serious contingency planning and backpacking may be in order.

- For multiple vehicles, the easiest and quickest solution would be to tow the disabled vehicle to the survival location or a good defendable site until it can be recovered. All vehicles should have tow straps. A good emergency tactical plan would be to have tow straps already hooked up to both the front and back of each vehicle, especially the trucks. All trucks in my group have winches on the front and tow straps on the back.

- Should the breakdown happen in a populated area where violence is possible, a quick reload to other vehicles would probably be best, but this depends on how critical the breakdown was. There are numerous situations where a breakdown would be catastrophic to the group making the move. Any breakdown is a tactical situation, and the group will be faced with immediate and life-changing decisions. When making any move, make sure you have adequate means to defend the move and, if necessary, extract the group and as much survival equipment as can be carried. If a vehicle is reloaded on another vehicle, make sure the fuel is drained from the tank and put into the other vehicles. If there is room on the other vehicles, you may want to take the wheels and any other parts that would come in handy.

Having read these tips, a good exercise would be to figure out what equipment you would need to accomplish those tasks. Plan, plan, and plan. No matter what you know you need, unless you have an extremely large group and functioning vehicles, you are never going to be able to carry or procure it all. You will quickly amass unmanageable tonnage. If in a rural or urban survival location, determine what you are going to have to do and what tools or equipment you need to do it. There are no good answers in these scenarios. Every group or individual must determine what is critical versus what's nice to have.

Ask Yourself What You Will Need to Have or Do

- Will I need books and reference data?
- Will I need to make location repairs?
- Will I need to fortify my location?
- Will I have to defend myself and others?
- Will I have to see at night?
- Will I need to make fires?
- Will I need to gather firewood?
- Will I need to sharpen axes and knives?
- Will I have to hunt game?
- Will I have to maintain and repair weapons?
- Will I have to process game?
- Will I have to cook?
- Will I have to can food?
- Am I going to fish for food?
- Will I grow a garden?
- Will I have to carry water?
- Will I have to trap rainwater?
- Will I have to purify water?
- Will group members get hurt?
- How will I care for them?
- Will I have to carry injured group members any distance?

- Will the group get infections or minor injuries?
- Will I need to control rodents?
- Will babies be born?
- Will I need warm clothes and bedding?
- Will I need extra footwear?
- Will I need to make or repair clothes?
- What can I hunt with to save ammunition?
- Will I have to build any survival structures, and will I have to make them waterproof?
- Will I need to tell direction?
- Will I have to carry heavy loads?
- Will I need rope and tie-downs?
- Will I need to clean myself and the living area?
- Will I need tools?
- Will I have to deal with human waste and garbage?
- Will I have to bury anyone who dies?
- Will I have to dig a hole?
- Where do we go if forced out of the survival location?
- What will I need to survive if forced out of the survival location?
- Where do I cache it?
- Will I have to survive extreme hot or cold weather?
- How much salt do I need per day?

Take this list and ask yourself what you will need to accomplish each task. Add to that food, water, fuel, guns, ammunition, and nice things to have that we have already discussed. Add this to what you already have on hand, and you are working on tonnage. The tools and items to ensure survival will take planning and preparation, and they will strain everyone's experience. I am not a prepper or hard-core survivalist, but I am experienced enough to plan for disaster. There are large military and civilian trucks for sale, and if you can purchase one, these would be an advantage for any planned trip to a rural survival site. If you have to go off-road, the higher the vehicle is off the ground with four-wheel drive, the better in my experience. To start realizing what it will take to operate in a remote rural area, get the group together and

One question that many people ask is if they can survive extreme hot or cold weather. (Dale C. Spartas/http://www.spartasphoto.com)

brainstorm your lists against what you have and what you need to get. Let's look at the first question on the list.

Question: Will I need books and reference data?
Answer: More than you can even imagine.

We are in the age of instant education; you can get any information at the touch of a finger. Once the power goes out and we find ourselves a couple hundred years back in history capability-wise, that is over. So let's put the thinking caps on as a group and start deciding what reference books would be good to have. I will put a list below for reference, and you will need to add the rest depending on your plans.

Good References to Have

- First aid and sanitation
- How to garden
- Land navigation
- Processing game
- Campfire cooking
- Weapons repair
- Caching
- Carpentry
- Canning
- Other ways to preserve food without refrigeration
- How to fish
- Survival books
- How to shoot
- Tactical manuals
- Maps
- Vehicle repair

Above is a good start, but the rest is up to you. A good reference library in a rural or urban area would be more than worth the effort it takes to put it together and transport it. Some references can be printed off the Internet and put into a three-ring binder, but books will last longer.

I said before, whether you are in a rural or urban location, everything nonperishable should be in packs or boxes and ready for quick loading into available transportation. If vehicles are not available, this transportation may be handcarts and similar equipment. If you have to head out with handcarts and your remote site is six hundred miles away, you probably won't make it for a couple of months or longer—if you make it at all. There might be an acceptable location closer, but you may have to start from scratch. However, the people who settled this country were often in the same situation.

Let's say you have done your homework on the above list, and you are ready to move if necessary. This will always be ongoing on the preparation side. An important part of that preparation is the visits to your rural survival site. One thing is certain: if there is vehicle access to the site and a structure on it, eventually it will be found and possibly broken into unless it is occupied full time. Nothing but everyday living materials should be there. Nothing should be there full time that you cannot afford to lose. Even in remote areas, there are opportunists or just bad apples.

Visits to the location should be spent becoming imminently familiar with the land and surrounding terrain. Any vegetation clearing for observation and defense purposes should be done and maintained. Potential cache sites should be picked and game availability assessed. Water sources should be evaluated and wood-gathering areas decided on. If you have had the rural site for any length of time, moving to it should be looked on as moving to a better place, but as discussed previously, if things go bad you must first survive the trip. I am most comfortable having a remote site I can get to with a single tank of fuel. Where I live, this is possible, but it is not for many of my friends who have a long way to go through many unknown circumstances.

When loading vehicles for the trip to the survival location, they should all be reverse loaded. This means long-term survival gear is loaded first and things needed upon arrival loaded last. Critical items, such as weapons, ammunition, tools, food, and water, should be cross-loaded onto different vehicles in case one or more vehicles are lost for whatever reason. This technique prevents the group from losing everything they need should disaster strike the move.

Groups who are moving to a survival property where no structures are on the site should pack their vehicles the same way. The
difference is in considering what they will need first in these circumstances. Are they going to initially build tents and then structures
or survival shelters? The trucks should be loaded appropriately. All
equipment not immediately needed should stay in the vehicles until
needed.

Circumstances may force a quick move even in a remote area, and
if supplies are unloaded and strewn about, the chance of losing a lot
of what you need is great. Never come back from a trip before disaster strikes without immediately filling all fuel tanks.

Let's say the move to the rural site went well and you are approach-
ing the area. Only own it for occupation once you prove no one is
waiting to ambush your arrival. We have discussed three options for
your survival location.

No Structure on the Location

Stop the vehicles at a predetermined point that is defendable and as
close as possible for an easy foot move. Half the group sets up security around the vehicles, and half the group makes a tactical move into
the initial site picked for occupation and makes a sweep to ensure it
is clear of ambushers. The site is kept under observation while the
trucks are contacted by whatever means are available and brought
forward. In a perfect world you would have radio communication,
but if not, couriers have to make the move on foot. Planning will
make this time-consuming operation more efficient.

The vehicles are then put into a defensive perimeter, and the initial site is prepared. I suggest waiting and observing the surrounding
areas or woods until you are satisfied that you are alone, then post
guards who continue to observe while the initial site is set up. All
tents or shelters should be inside the vehicle perimeter. Vehicles
become initial cover if looters or raiders fire on you. The group
should plan to arrive at the rural site early in the morning so you
have a full day to set up and establish 24/7 security. Stopping in a
close, defendable location if it's getting late is a good plan. Secure
yourself that night, then make an early morning tactical move into
the site to give yourself a full day to set up your initial site.

Structure Unoccupied on Property

This property should be occupied the same way as a property with no structure on it. The only difference is that the structure should be tactically cleared to ensure it is empty. All other protocols are in place—with the exception that you have a structure to occupy and vehicles should be pulled up to the house so they can be covered by guards. Twenty-four-seven security operations for the group start on arrival at the site. A good technique for seeing if anyone has been on your property is to install trail cameras to monitor the area during one of your visits.

Structure on Site Occupied by Group Members

This should be the easiest if plans are in place and everyone knows the plan. Upon arrival, a few group members dismount and make contact with the on-site members by an arranged signal. Then bring up the vehicles and begin occupying the site. A second option is that vehicles drive up to an arranged site, recognition signals are verified, vehicles move onto the site, and security and move-in operations are started. There should be a duress signal that is known by all that the occupying group members and arriving members know. This is in the event that the site is taken over by looters or raiders and they are waiting in ambush. Being in the business I have been in, I would stop the vehicles close to the site in a good defensible position and send three or four group members forward to observe the site undetected for a few hours to ensure all is well. I have occasionally been called paranoid for thinking this way, but it has saved my life in critical situations on two occasions. You will have to make the decision to do what you think is best after reading this book. In the event of a disaster, I hope this book gives you good options you may not have previously thought of. In the end, you will live or die by the decisions you make. I live in a rural state and have left my house vacant for a year at a time and have never had any problems. With this in mind, will I be able to do that after disaster strikes? I think not.

In my life, I have been in some of the most remote areas in this country and the world. I have been in most mountainous areas in Montana, Wyoming, North Carolina, and Washington State; I have been in Louisiana swamps, Georgia mountains, and Tennessee hills.

On numerous occasions I have thought I was twenty to fifty miles away from any human, but that thought was generally proven wrong by a myriad of hunters, backpackers, hikers, campers, geologists, forest rangers, etc. Your rural survival spot, no matter how remote, is known by a lot more people than you think.

It is a given that if disaster strikes, you are going to have to defend yourself from people trying to get what you have. You will have to do this more in urban areas due to the amount of people in your location. In rural areas, you must keep the same security protocols as in the city, but the chance of dealing with people who may not be a threat is better. That does not mean you can take a security break— stay ready and on guard. The difference in rural areas is that there are numerous people who can take care of themselves and know how to survive on their own in a survival situation. You will have people approach you that may want to join the group. You may have people ask the group for help. This could happen in urban areas, as well. In the group's planning and preparation, the group rules for interacting with other people during survival or disaster situations should fall along these lines no matter where you are—in your survival location or out gathering. Failure to follow these rules will sooner or later result in disaster for the group.

The Rules

- Every contact with others is a tactical situation.
- People are not trusted until they prove themselves.
- Anyone taken in by the group must be an asset and lend something to the group.
- No sick, injured, or mentally disturbed people.
- No deadweight—if they do not conform to group rules, deal with them quickly.
- Only take in numbers you can watch, guard, or vet that they are what they say.
- Do not let them have weapons until they prove themselves.
- Be careful in all situations; control your immediate and surrounding space. The chance of making bad decisions is good, so watch out for slick talkers who try to get a portion of the group into a specific area. If it sounds too good to be true, it most likely isn't a good choice.
- While in your rural hide, there will be danger areas. The first is the location where you are set up, so guard it 24/7 or pay the price. The other danger areas should be moved into and worked in tactically.

Other Danger Areas

- Latrines

- Wood-gathering areas

- Water-gathering areas, including bathing areas

- Dump, burial, or burn sites

- Game-processing areas

- Hunting areas, such as tree stands or blinds

- Any movement outside the main location

The bottom line is that a group member should always be watching the back of workers. The duties should be rotated regularly. I cannot tell you how many Viet Cong, Taliban, Al Qaeda, and other bad guys around the world have died quickly by not securing themselves in critical situations because they thought they were safe. If disaster strikes on a grand scale, the rest of your life may be spent in a critical situation. It's your call on what your life is worth and what you are willing to do to preserve it. The percentage of us who are prepared will live or die like everyone else by following or ignoring the rules. It's easy to drop your guard when you think you're safe or when security becomes routine. That is exactly what raiders and looters are looking for when they are on the prowl. Always keep in mind that you and your group are not the only ones armed and planning.

I have put out advance copies of this book for friends to review, and some said civilians reading this might not know some of the tactics I have posted. I agree, and that is why prior preparation and training are critical. No one knows when disaster of epic circumstances will happen, so now is the time to start preparing. This book cannot possibly address all the preparation and training needs of millions of individuals. It will, however, give you a start. Within the country, there are millions of veterans who served in combat arms during their service. Most people know at least one of these veterans, and that's a good start. At the rear of this book, I will also include a list of training and shooting schools that will assist your efforts. To put everything that could be done to prepare for unknown disasters into this book would produce a document so heavy it could not be lifted. The lists I have provided so far will give any group a good start. Go over the lists as a group item by item, and list what you have versus what you need for equipment and training. Start now, the clock is ticking.

One of the most important things a group in a remote location should be paying attention to is signs that other people are present. One thing that is helpful is for group members to have the same soles on boots and running shoes so outside tracks can be detected. Noises, such as talking, gunshots, and woodcutting, should be listened for. Group members should also pick different pieces of terrain where large tracts of the property and surrounding land can be observed with binoculars and hopefully provide early warning of outsider approach.

Some dogs will benefit security and generally give early warning, but they will have to be fed. A good plan if this is a long-term survival situation is to have males and females that can breed. If the food situation gets bad, you can always reduce your early warning capability by enhancing your food supply.

I have seen several properties that friends are planning to use as survival locations. With one exception, all were well thought out and had an abundance of trees for firewood and water on the location. Firewood and water are imperative for survival, especially in states with harsh winters. Land with hills will provide shelter from high winds and long-range observation of the location but will allow close approach to the site by anyone entering the property. No matter how bad you

Water is imperative for survival. (Dale C. Spartas/http://www.spartasphoto.com)

would like to stay on the site without being found, your occupation of the site will ensure your detection by anyone in the immediate, and possibly adjoining, areas.

Look around at surrounding terrain. If you can see far hills, you can be seen by anyone on them. Smoke from cooking or warming fires can be seen and smelled at long ranges. No matter how big or small the group may be, the very act of moving to collect water, firewood, and game will leave well-worn trails that will lead to the site. Gardens will be a giveaway of close habitation, as will garbage dumps or burn sites. The bottom line is that you will be found—probably sooner than later. Let's keep it simple with security: there is either a problem imminent, a potential problem, or things are normal. Groups can use whatever security protocols they wish. The following status of security is just a guide.

Group Security Status

Normal

- Everyone sleeps—two or three guards are always watching.
- Work parties are out—a guard is watching.
- Everyone is eating—two or three guards are watching.
- Visitors show up—two or three guards are watching.

Potential Problem

- Two-thirds of the group sleep or work and are armed—one-third guards.
- This can be modified depending on group capability and knowledge of the situation.

Problem Imminent

- Half sleep or work and are armed—half guards.

This is as simple as it gets. When attacked or if a direct, active threat presents itself, all hands are on deck at determined defensive positions. Groups will use whatever security protocols they believe they need. These will be based on site location, group size, threat to the group, terrain surrounding the location, and the group's ability to deal with the situation effectively. If there are hills close to your rural survival location, it is probable that you will be observed by anyone interested in the location, and any attack on your location will either come from those hills, be supported from those hills, or both. You will be operating at all times in a potential problem status once disaster happens. The amount of people who may be moving into remote areas could be excessive the closer the area is to large population centers.

I have a large high hill that starts in my backyard and goes up on a 30 percent uniform slope for one hundred and fourteen yards to the crest. The side of the hill has a few bushes; the top of the hill has seventy yards along the crest of thick mountain mahogany bushes. There are no bushes on the hill that are not periodically and selectively trimmed. Anyone in those bushes is backlit by the cuttings so while in the bushes, you would never know you had an issue unless you were very well trained. People who I have sent there to observe or look through their scopes come under one heading: easily identifiable targets. You may not want to go to this extreme, but you should be able to control your surrounding areas out to three hundred yards at least.

When planning and visiting your rural survival area, this discussion is one of the preparation points that should be accomplished. All the tactical planning should have the objective of making it hard for looters or raiders to be successful against you. Any preparation of terrain should focus on what you can do to make easy targets out of the people attacking you. We have been talking about group security and protecting the survival location. We are discussing rural locations in this chapter, but it should not be lost on anyone that true security and safety is attained by a large well-prepared group. I will just state facts here; groups will have to accomplish all we have discussed in this book. The smaller the group, the less chance you will have of being successful.

Things That Will Cause Group Failure

- Lack of planning, preparation, and training
- Not adhering religiously to tactical and security protocols
- Attrition of the group through casualties
- Group sickness due to neglecting good sanitation requirements
- Dissent, infighting, or traitors in the group
- Failure to successfully hunt and gather food and water

- Failure to prepare and stock up for a harsh winter
- Making bad tactical and security decisions

There are certainly other things that can be added to the list, but if these factors are in order, the chance of the group surviving will be above average in any catastrophic national disaster that causes a long-term survival situation. In a remote rural area, part of security is looking for signs daily that tell you that you are not alone.

Signs to Look or Listen For

- Footprints crossing your normal routes of movement
- If vehicles are working, any unknown vehicle tracks
- Horse tracks
- Campfires the group didn't make
- Shelters the group didn't make
- Digging or woodcutting the group didn't do
- Gunshots
- Signs of dressing animals the group didn't kill
- Hunting arrows the group didn't shoot
- Missing items from storage areas or gardens
- Human voices
- Sounds of woodcutting
- Barking dogs not owned by the group
- Strangers moving around the property

If you are paying attention to the above list, you should not be surprised by visitors or attackers. If any of the above signs are close to the survival structures, you need to accept that you have been found. The first question should be why they did not make contact. Raise the group's security level considerably, and start some patrols around to see what may be going on and coming at you.

This would be a group call based on what has been found or detected and what they know should be going on around them. There is no good news here. Know what is going on around you, stay alert and on guard, or pay the price. This too is a group call. I have talked about injured and deadweight group members. Family groups with these members will have to make their own decisions. Those decisions will be difficult and life-changing, but you must look at it from a life or death survival situation. Do you keep a family member who may cause the group to fail, or do you get rid of him or her by throwing them out of the group? This is a hard call, and no one can make it but the affected group. Of course, injured group members in good standing can do light guard duty at the survival location. Removing unwanted family members from the group would by no means set a precedent.

Part of your group preparation should be considering who should be in the group. Both family groups and nonfamily groups that were formed due to the situation will have problems dealing with people who may be a hindrance to the group. If in normal time before the disaster strikes there is dislike for a person, this is not going to get better once disaster strikes and things get critical and life-threatening. I will leave this subject by saying groups will fare much better if they are a close, functional group with no deadweight members.

In a rural area while in a survival situation, people in the group are going to get hurt. Before the disaster, it's a simple act to transport them to the emergency room or call an ambulance on your cell phone. This is not going to happen if disaster strikes. While in a remote area, we are basically on our own and stuck with having to deal with medical emergencies with what we have at hand. If the group has trained EMTs or doctors with equipment, that is great. If they do not, some serious training and equipping during preparation is required. Realistically, if you have serious medical emergencies, you are probably going to watch group members die as a result of those emergencies. There is no good news here. In a later chapter, we will talk about equipment and cover the medical equipment that is available and will do a good job taking care of minor injuries, but very few of them take care of serious injuries, such as gunshot wounds. Yes, you can bandage the wound and maybe stop the bleeding, but gunshot wounds require surgery. Unless you have a trained surgeon, you are dead in the water for saving the group member who is critically injured.

In all groups, there will be members who are looking for perfect answers. After the disaster there will be none, and if you realistically look at what has taken place before the disaster you will quickly real-ize there are no guarantees. Family members or group members only have to take a look at what has happened in their lives when times were good: how many vehicle accidents with injuries have happened and how many trips there were to the emergency room for bad cuts, broken bones, or the flu. All these will continue to happen after the disaster. The reality will be that you will most likely have to deal with them at the group level, especially in a remote environment.

If you go back two hundred years, people living in remote areas were left mainly to their own devices. In modern society, we have gotten used to running to Wal-Mart or the emergency room when things are needed or go bad. This should be well understood by all planning a move to a remote location. You will be on your own. A knee-jerk response will be to stock up on medical equipment. This is a good idea, but it is effort wasted if trained personnel to use the equipment are not available. It is easy to say, but attention to detail goes a long way in preventing sickness, such as having warm clothes in the winter and staying dry and out of the wind. Groups need to realize that in a remote area, sooner or later you are going to run out of everything, and you will truly be forced to live off the land.

Chapter Four

The Individual Survivor

I would like to think that this book, as well as other survival books and websites, will convince a large part of the population to start to prepare. If this does take place, there will still be hundreds of thousands, if not millions, who will start out any disaster alone. I know several individuals who are preparing to do just that. I have stated previously that individuals will have a hard time surviving—more so in an urban environment than a rural one. Can a lone individual survive on his or her own in a survival situation that may last years? The answer is certainly yes, and there is data to support this. Get on the Internet and reference Eric Rudolph of North Carolina. This individual was wanted by law enforcement for an abortion clinic bombing. He was on the run in remote areas for five years before being arrested by a deputy while looking for food in a dumpster. He did it in a remote area that he had intimate knowledge of and had prepared, but he was finally pushed into a patrolled area and was caught. A lot of the time, he evaded well-trained law enforcement officers with dogs. Eventually he just ran out of food. There are reports that he occasionally had help from friends and was given shelter and food, but this notwithstanding, he proved it could be done in a remote area under severe restrictions.

In 2014, we had Eric Matthew Frein, who was accused of ambushing two Pennsylvania state troopers—allegedly killing one and wounding the other. Frein went into a remote area that he had spent years preparing. He evaded hundreds of law enforcement officers who looked for him. Their search turned up prepared booby traps and caches of food, equipment, weapons, and ammunition. Obviously he prepared well. Nevertheless, as predicted during the writing of this book, US Marshals apprehended Eric Frein on October 30, 2014.

Even If Trained, Experienced, and Prepared, These Things Work Against an Individual

- He will eventually have to move outside the hide.
- He will leave tracks or signs.
- He will most likely be seen in an urban area.
- His supplies will have to be replaced fairly quickly.
- Eventually he will have to hunt and cook what he acquires.
- He will have to pass human waste and hide it.
- He may get sick or hurt.
- In harsh winters, he will have to build a fire.
- He will have to carry everything he needs on his back or a cart.
- If anyone is hunting him, they will eventually find him or he will walk into them while moving.

This list just about guarantees an individual will run into people. It will be quicker in an urban area because of the mass of people that will be moving around. In a rural setting, the bigger the area the individual has to move in, the longer he may last, but eventually his luck will run out.

If you are going to prepare an area for individual survival, you need to make a list of what you may have to do and the equipment you will need to do it. If you look at it realistically, the list will not differ much from the one in Chapter Three. There are some glaring differences, as the individual survivor will not be able to depend on guards and group support. Put that up against the fact that he will have to sleep, and you can see that there will be a constant pressure of finding a place to sleep that is secure. Just the capability of finding a secure place and determining that you are not being followed by someone who has seen you is a time-consuming and never-ending task. Additionally, that place will have to change regularly lest you leave worn trails, which will lead others to you. Many things must be determined by the individual survivor if there is to be any chance of him lasting any amount of time.

He Must First Pick His Area and Determine

- Are there hide places where I will be secure?
- How many cache sites will I need?
- Are they available on the terrain I have picked?
- Can I survive a harsh winter?
- If I have to hunt game, can I do it silently?
- Are there water sources available?
- Are there places I can build a fire with multiple escape routes if detected?
- What if my cache sites are found?
- Can I find a site for a long-term stay if it snows?
- Can I stock it for the stay?
- What will I need to carry if found and forced out of the area?

The individual is in a lot of trouble if other people are around the area and looking for food, water, or any survival equipment they can find regardless of if they are in a rural or urban setting. Now let's modify the planning list in Chapter Three for the individual. Remember the constants: he will have to eat, sleep, and drink water, and he will need fire and shelter.

A Planning List for an Individual's Cache

- Will I need books and reference data?
- Will I have to build survival shelters in adverse weather?
- Will I have to see at night?
- Will I have to make fires?
- Will I have to dig a hole?

- Will I or can I grow a garden?
- Will I have to gather firewood?
- Will I have to cook?
- Will I have to sharpen axes and knives?
- Will I have to hunt game?
- Will I have to maintain and repair weapons?
- Will I have to process game?
- Will I have to fish?
- Will I have to carry water?
- Will I have to trap rainwater?
- Will I have to purify water?
- What do I need if I am hurt or sick?
- Will I get infections or minor injuries?
- Will I need warm clothes and bedding?
- Will I need extra footwear?
- Will I need to make or repair clothes?
- What do I need to hunt silently?
- Will I need to tell direction?
- Will I need to carry heavy loads?
- Will I need rope and tie-downs?
- Will I need to clean myself and my clothes?
- How do I get rid of waste and garbage?
- Where do I go if forced out of my chosen location?
- What will I need to survive if forced out of location?
- Where do I cache it?
- What do I need on my person and in caches to protect myself?
- How much salt will I need per day, and where do I get it?

You can see why Eric Frein took years to prepare his remote area. Obviously, he was not totally successful in caching because the law enforcement officers searching for him found some of them, or he was careless in picking his hide sites. Anyone contemplating individual survival in any rural or remote area is taking on a job he cannot be successful in for the long term—at least to where he is comfortable. If you look at the planning list and figure what equipment it entails, along with the equipment weight—not to mention keeping track of and finding the right cache sites—you certainly would need years to accomplish this task. You would also need to take the time to know the area intimately.

One thing that will get you ambushed is that you will have to visit your cache sites regularly, and this will eventually wear an observable trail right to the site. In urban areas, you may not make as many trails, but you will make few movements without someone observing you, especially in the early days of the disaster. As time goes by and more and more hungry people are moving around—most likely in groups—the chance of running into them, possibly at close range, is almost ensured. Also, as an individual you may be incapable of the logistic efforts required to cache and the tactical requirements to ensure their protection.

Whatever terrain you pick to sleep in a rural area must be somewhere people would not generally go—and never at night. The terrain you pick for survival should be heavily wooded, mountainous, and remote. Places picked for sleeping should be in the thickest vegetation you can find. If a survival shelter must be built due to inclement weather, it will be hidden, and anyone moving in the area after dark will certainly make noise. In urban terrain, your sleeping area should be where you will not be found. Intimate knowledge of what is happening around you and buildings or available areas will be mandatory and still may not keep you secure. If anyone in what would be hundreds of buildings saw you, I can guarantee you will have visitors you do not want. In rural terrain, the surrounding hills are your enemy, as anyone on them with binoculars will see you and move on you.

In an urban setting, I cannot see a lone individual surviving for any length of time without running into people who would want to do him harm. With that being said, if the individual knows his area of movement and has watched the movement of other people in the vicinity, he may last a long time before luck runs out. For example, I have spent years moving about urban areas where detection was not in my best interest. I can say without reservation that from about three in the morning until around five or six, you can get away with almost anything. In areas where combat is taking place, there are always guards on duty that you may run into. In a survival situation, a lot of people, for a myriad of reasons from hunger to sickness to worry, would not be sleeping regularly and would be watching the streets. Many may not care that they see someone moving, and you would have no issues. However, others, especially a group, would wonder what you might be carrying and if they could use it. In rural terrain, many people who cannot sleep may use the darkness to move around while feeling secure in their movements.

Planning your route in an urban area at any time, even if meticulously planned and executed, may not be enough if large amounts of people are observing from the many buildings. The chance of

In a rural setting, observe with binoculars before moving to your next point on the ground. (Dale C. Spartas/http://www.spartasphoto.com)

running into a group or individual you do not want to meet is almost assured. Planning your route in a rural area if you know people are near is just as important. Moving undetected requires planning, skill, and knowledge of the terrain.

In a rural setting, properly planned movement will work most of the time if you are using the terrain properly, moving slowly, and observing with binoculars before moving to your next point on the ground. Staying off present trails, staying in shadows, and using the vegetation to your advantage works most of the time—even with many people looking for you. Most people who decide to go the individual route of survival do not have other people they know to form a group, do not trust people, or are afraid of people. No matter what the reason is that they decided to go it alone, they have chosen a path that is problematic every day for the duration of the situation. Just determining what they are going to carry with them day to day may decide their fate.

If it's summer, winter clothes and bedding will not be needed, and just food, water, and protective gear can be carried. If it's winter, the load on the individual goes up. There are good and bad things about preparing your survival area with caches. With caches of support equipment and sustenance, things can be easier as long as what you have stored lasts, but these caches also tie you to the area. They become your personal store for everything. If, for whatever reason, the caches are found or you are run out of the area, you will go immediately to surviving with what you are carrying and what game you can acquire. One good thing is that with a disaster, a certain percentage of the population will move or evacuate quickly, and in an urban area this will assure numerous structures for temporary shelter. In rural areas, any structure will have to be fabricated from existing materials. These needed survival structures will also key other people into your presence.

In this chapter on individual survival actions, I will bounce back and forth from urban to rural areas as I think of situations. You will notice, as with the rest of the book, this chapter seems to have no structure; however, it is full of critical information for survival.

If an individual is out and moving, he should be carrying a pack that will sustain him for at least seventy-two hours or more. Small military units go out into remote, dangerous areas with packs that sustain them for a week or more. The reason an individual should have this equipment with him is in the event that he has to evade a group and cannot get back to his hide. In addition to protective gear, the pack should contain food, water, shelter, and fire-making materials. I have learned from my military survival training, as well as books I have read, that it is pretty much a given that these are the four essentials to support life. This holds true in the urban or rural setting. For example, in an urban area if it's below zero outside, eventually in buildings with no services it will become below zero inside, as well.

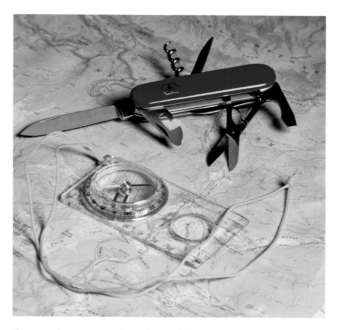

A map and compass are two of several items you should never travel without during a disaster. (Dale C. Spartas/http://www.spartasphoto.com)

Regardless of what is in your pack, never travel without your guns, ammunition, compass, and binoculars. If the individual does not find food and water once he runs out of what he is carrying or has cached, he is on borrowed time. He will rapidly weaken, become ineffective, and start making mistakes that will most likely get him killed before he starves to death or dies of dehydration. If disaster strikes, there will be numerous individuals who will try to go it alone. This will probably only end in disaster, but the world is full of stories of people who have been lost in the wild for weeks and survived by eating bugs and worms and drinking out of mud puddles. This is not a good life, but it is life and with that there is always luck and hope.

With a lot of luck and experience, an individual with a little equipment and knowledge could last a long time. One of the things Rudolph and Frein did was find people's gardens or stored food and took it while they were gone or asleep. In a long-term survival situation, I am sure if that chance presented itself to the individual, he would take advantage of it. I am also sure whoever he took it from would not be happy and would go looking for him. I suggest you stock up as much as you can and then put distance between you and whomever you looted. In the end, what the individual loots from others is good survival practice, but chasing him down and killing him is a natural survival reaction.

An individual who wants to be alone and stay away from other people will probably fail and be found if he is in an area where winters are cold and long. He will not want to get wet, he will want to stay out of the wind, and he will need a fire daily. That fire will provide lifesaving warmth, but it will also send a possibly life-ending signal to looters or raiders.

Problems with Fires

- Anyone downwind will smell it.
- If it's smoky, anyone close or in the line of sight will see it.
- At night, the glare will be seen by anyone in the line of sight.
- At night, vision outside the cone of light is made more difficult.
- Unless the fire residue can be hidden, people will have a starting point to track you.

These points are true and have gotten combat soldiers and civilians in combat areas killed all over the world. Nevertheless, in a winter environment, a fire will be essential to survival. If the individual has the right bedding to survive the night, he could build fires only in the daytime. He may be able to build a mainly smoke-free fire if he has the right wood. He may find a good dry streambed or gully to build a small warming fire in and not be detected. In any case, the need for a daily fire requires the gathering of wood, which raises the chance of being found considerably. A lifesaving fire in winter while people are looking to do you harm is a double-edged sword; it can get you killed while saving your life.

Another problem for the individual in winter is that once it snows, anyone can find his tracks. Deep snow may restrict his movement, make wood gathering difficult, and escape, if found, virtually impossible. If he should be injured or become sick to the point where he cannot take care of himself, he will surely die. Here, as in a lot of life or death situations, there is no good news.

Another weakness for the individual—and they are numerous—is that he must cache ammunition for his weapons and hope they are not found. If he is carrying seventy-two hours of sustaining equipment, he is going to be limited on the ammunition he can carry. He can offset this problem by either caching or going the .22 rifle route. If he is carrying a .22, he can carry hundreds of rounds with him. I suggest the individual survivor also have a bow and arrow for silent hunting. There are excellent fold-up bows that would fit any survival situation. Crossbows are also a good close-range silent weapon. The problem with crossbows and compound bows is if they break, they require tools and repair parts. These can, of course, be cached, but I personally prefer a simple recurve bow with extra strings carried in my pack. The choice of anything, including bow and weapons, must be an individual's choice. I may recommend something that might not be the best choice all around, but it is the best choice for me.

No matter what the individual decides he needs, he is not going to be able to carry it all. Good locations for cache sites will need to be picked or created, and multiple trips to your cache site will eventually leave a trail right to it. The best way to cache is to store several things in it you will need to survive, and when the time comes where you need it, visit the cache site one time and clean it out. If someone finds the location dug up and empty, all they have is a dug up and empty cache site.

Let's talk about a true survival situation as it pertains to the individual. I want people reading this book to understand what I am saying about individual survival and the range of possible disasters and successes the individual faces. If you have read this chapter up to this point, you have already got a lot of information on what faces an individual in a survival situation. If he is in a remote area and there is no one else for miles, his survival depends on his skills and his ability to gather food and water, to get a fire going, and to build a survival shelter to protect himself from the weather. It also depends on what gear he has with him and how proficient he is with it. In an urban situation, it will eventually boil down to how clever, well prepared, and lucky he is.

The next situation I can see is that the individual is in a long-term survival situation in either an urban or rural setting and there are other people in close proximity. In this situation, the individual who wants or has to stay away from others is dependent on how well prepared he is and how adept he is at staying away from the others. Several things will be in play that will affect the end game one way or the other. The first is that everyone in the area, whether a group or individuals, will be in a live-or-die survival situation. They will also be in competition with each other for any available food, water, fire, or shelter needs. In this scenario, everyone is trying to survive, and no one has the time to spend looking for the other survivors. This is where luck comes in and an individual may not be found or walk into the others. Therefore, he continues to do what he has to do to survive. This situation is one where I believe a move will be forced on everyone who is physically able as the area's food sources are depleted.

A third situation would be where the previous situation is taking place but there are groups that are big enough that while part of the group is gathering what the group needs to survive, the other part of the group is dedicated to roving the area to find other survivors and loot what they have. This would be the most dangerous for the individual survivor and would quickly force him to move his location or join up with a group for protection. If this part of the book does nothing else, I hope it sheds a little light on the folly of trying to make it alone. Planning is mandatory for the individual, but very quickly the cards are going to be stacked against him in situations where other people or groups are around.

One thing the individual has going for him is that most untrained groups do not know how to search a piece of land, either urban or rural, and are operating under a false sense of superiority. If an individual is observing the space around him before moving and is using well-prepared hide sites, he has a good chance of staying away from those pursuing him. Go back and reread the dangers of making fires and traveling in snow, as these are the big dangers that will lead people to you, along with gunshots if you cannot hunt silently.

One of the misconceptions that a lot of folks have is that the remote areas are full of game for hunting. This is true in some areas, but in others there is almost nothing to catch. You only need to look at some of the reality survival shows on TV to see how hard or impossible it is to catch anything to eat on a regular basis. If a national disaster strikes, forcing everyone to survive on what they can find in both urban and rural areas, what food or game exists will rapidly be depleted. Here, as in other situations described in this book, there is no good news.

Let's talk about hide sites. There are several theories on what makes a hide site. One, it should be in a place that is extremely hard to find or get to. In rural areas, use the thickest vegetation you can find. You can also dig it in or find a hill with a cut in it. I have gotten under a low growing spruce tree in an area that was not heavily vegetated and watched several people look for me and not find me. I was in a good camouflaged ghillie suit and blended well with the tree I was under. The bottom line is that hide sites work, but they must either not be found or blend in with their surroundings. In some vegetation, you can get under it without leaving a trace of your presence. This comes under the heading of find a hole and pull it over you. This is using camouflage, the art of blending in, to its maximum. Do not forget, camouflage is a stationary art, so movement is easily detected. Some people think that putting on a camouflage suit and painting your face means you can move around without being detected.

In my time, I have trained many hundreds of military and police snipers and recon personnel, and all have heard this statement from me: "The best camouflaged man in the world who is moving looks just like the best camouflaged man in the world moving." Movement is instantly detected by anyone watching in both urban and rural environments. Some terrain looks like nothing could hide in it. Areas that come to mind are the Yakima desert area in eastern Washington State, the high desert areas of eastern Montana and Wyoming, the wheat fields of Kansas, and other similar places. But if you get out and walk these areas, there are millions of folds in the ground, some bushes, holes, and dry streambeds where many people could hide from ground observation. Standing up and moving would be instantly detected by anyone looking into that area, but hide sites do abound.

It would also help if your clothes were the same color as the surrounding vegetation. Keep in mind that hide sites that are detected can be moved on and surrounded, so careful selection and minimum to no movement during daylight hours is imperative. Another thing the individual should do when picking any remote site is spending the time to find one with water, game, hills, and vegetation that will support his intentions. The time and money spent doing this will pay dividends in the future.

If an individual is going to make the decision to go it alone if disaster strikes, he has taken on a monumental challenge that will ultimately end in disaster. Luck and skill has a lot to do with it. American history is full of stories about lone mountain men who survived against incredible dangers by luck, skill, and their personal daring. I do not take the lone lifestyle, but if others do then I say good travels and good luck—just make sure you plan and prepare.

One thing that happens a lot in critical situations is that group members will get split up from the main group. All group members should know this may happen as a result of losing your way, getting separated in the dark, as a result of a gunfight, inclement weather, or a myriad of other things. The bad news is that whether it takes hours, days, or weeks to regain contact with the group, you are alone and surviving as a lone person—all of the things we have discussed in this

Some terrain looks like nothing could hide in it. The wheat fields of Kansas is one such place that comes to mind. (Ricardo Reitmeyer, courtesy of iStock)

chapter may begin to affect you to some extent, most assuredly if it's winter and people are looking to do you harm. This is why I have stated that when traveling outside the survival location, you should be carrying what you need to survive and protect yourself for at least three days, or seventy-two hours. Failure to follow that simple combat rule could mean you do not make it through the night.

A fatal mistake made throughout history by men in critical situations is to assume that you can cut corners and not take everything required. Men have died and military units have been destroyed or hurt badly by those assumptions. All should be aware that in critical situations, things will go wrong—probably at the worst possible time. As in most things in life, failure to use good sense or not following the rules will ultimately get you in trouble. In survival situations, it could mean a fatal error. This could be an error that is not seen because of assumptions, such as:

- We are only going a short distance and will be back in an hour.
- I do not need my warm clothes because we will be moving.
- I can leave my pack here, as we will not need what's in it.

Now that you are separated from the group and herded away from the survival site by looters, it's getting dark and it's below zero. You are alone without the right clothes, the ability to start a fire, or shelter from the cold and wind. The initial assumption was bad. The violation of leaving equipment behind will most likely prove fatal, but the assumption always makes sense until things go wrong or not as planned.

This scenario has played itself out many times in the past with soldiers in combat, hunters in remote areas, backpackers in mountain states—all have perished from making the incorrect decision or not following established protocols. If disaster strikes and you are forced to travel outside the survival location, never do so without your total survival and protective gear. Seventy-two hours is not long, but it is more than enough time to kill you under adverse conditions if you have not prepared correctly. People reading this might think this is a little harsh, but I will say to those people if you have not lived it and had to endure it, believe me, it is not harsh. It is sound tactical and survival advice, as I have no dog in anyone's fight except my own. If you break the rules in critical situations, you will pay the price. Ask any professional.

Chapter Five

Getting Ready

If you are extremely wealthy and can buy and stock your urban or rural location to make it into an impregnable fortress, then life is good, go do it. But, keep in mind that no matter how much you stock up, eventually you will run out and have to get your hands dirty. For the rest of us, if we are already preparing and planning, we are on the road to getting where we think we need to go. For those among us that are just waking up to the fact that some preparation is a good idea, you have a daunting task in front of you. If you don't have the funds to get what you need immediately, you are looking at a task that will take some time and require good organization, planning, and focus.

In saying that, the first thing most regular folks who are living paycheck to paycheck have to do is make some tough decisions. If I have to get certain items, what can I cut every week to get what I need to start preparing? First make an inventory of what you have. No matter what you get or have in your possession now, if disaster strikes you are going to have to defend yourself and what you have with your current supplies. If you live in an urban area, this may be quicker than you think. In most storm-related disasters, looting has started during the storm. If you are one of the antigun group and a person who believes in the good of their fellow man—I will be as politically correct as I can here—get some guns and ammunition you damned idiot. There, I have put some political correctness into this book. If you own guns, this is a start regardless of what type they are. Make sure they work and you have cleaning gear for them, as well as ammunition.

My recommendation is to start buying a box of ammunition for your currently owned guns every week or month. Have the people in your group who own guns do the same. Do a group inventory of what you have on hand now and available to the group if disaster happens in the near future. The group may be in better shape than you think. Put all ammunition in packs that can be picked up and moved quickly. You read my weapon suggestions in Chapter One, but do not spend a lot of money you do not have. Sometimes pawn-shops have some of the cheapest guns; get a good combat pistol with extra magazines and a shotgun if you do not have one. Another thing is knives, which you will use as tools and maybe defensive weapons. Look first in your kitchen knife drawer; most of us have knives that would be excellent in a survival situation.

We will talk more about what knives and tools you may need later in this chapter. As a side note, if you pick some kitchen knives for survival work, you will need to make or buy sheaths to carry them safely. As you prepare and go over the lists in this book and on the Internet, the group needs to determine what items are needed and who in the group can procure them. This will keep the group, which may be short on funds, from buying twenty sledgehammers when two would do it.

The next thing is food. You are already buying food, so start buying an extra bag of dry beans, rice, or canned food. Rotate the canned food, and continue to eat the oldest cans first. Continue to buy extra nonperishable food that can be prepared by adding water. There are many survival tips on how to do this on the websites for the Department of Homeland Security and FEMA, in addition to some excellent survival blogs.

This will be an ongoing protocol. If this were a perfect world, and I know it's not, all nonperishable foods would come in or be put into packs or boxes for easy movement. Keep in mind what you have stored for survival versus your ability to move it. For example, if you have enough equipment to fill a pickup truck and you own a Volkswagen, you do not have the room to pack what you have to move. This needs to be looked at from the group level, as well. Can we move ourselves and our supplies with the vehicles we have? If the answer is no, what are the group's options? One answer may be pooling money for a bigger vehicle—think a truck with four-wheel drive. The best trucks would be military trucks that come up for sale at different venues. Do not buy these blindly—go look at them and make sure you are not purchasing a vehicle that has reached the end of its days and will not survive the trip to your rural survival site. We will talk more about this later—right now I am trying to get some thinking going for an inexperienced group.

The next thing is water. There is a lot of good advice on the storage of water. If you are planning to get out of town when disaster strikes, filling up your bathtub with water is a waste of time, but you should still do it in case of unplanned changes. I am an old guy who says store it in five-gallon cans, rotate it at least twice a year by watering your plants or washing your car, and keep it out of direct sunlight. Also, if water is cut off with no notice, are there water sources near you that can provide water? Any water obtained from lakes, streams, or ponds should be boiled before drinking; if it's muddy it should be filtered until clear.

This book is on how to Survive While Surviving and how to prepare to do it. How to do it is already so available and redundant that I would be wasting my time, as well as yours, by putting it into this book. The next thing is the making of fire, and most people will buy lighters or matches. In my experience, if lighters are stored long term, the fuel will eventually leach out, especially after being used. Standard matches should not be bought. Sporting goods stores and survival shops sell matches that can be used under adverse conditions and are packed in weatherproof wrappings; these are what should be purchased and stored for emergency use.

I suggest rereading the list in Chapter Three to review what equipment is needed. These are lists to make an individual or group that is planning to survive sit down and think about what they will need to accomplish the stated tasks. Keep track of what you are acquiring and storing versus your capability to move it. Remember, if it's a planned move, do you have the vehicle space to move it in one load? If you are not planning to move and are going to use your residence as your survival location, what is the plan if you are forced out by extreme circumstances?

Extreme Circumstances

- Riots in your neighborhood.
- Your house is set on fire by looters.
- Flooding or wildfires in the area where you live.
- Time goes by and your resources are depleted.
- Sickness and diseases are breaking out due to sanitation failure.

You get the idea. Whatever it is that forces you to move is irrelevant. It has forced a move with all its attending circumstances, many of which are discussed in Chapter Three. Let's keep on the track of the regular guy and his family preparing. I have no idea what room is available to each individual who has decided to do some preparation, but I am assuming that if they are living in anything like a one- to three-bedroom structure, storage room will be at a premium. I know people who have made some hard decisions, such as designating their cellar, one of their bedrooms, or their garage as the place they will store what they are gathering. If they plan on staying in their residence as their survival location, this will work as long as they are not forced out by circumstances previously discussed.

If they are planning to move to another location when disaster strikes and they have a vehicle to load it into, will they have time to do this once things start happening? The best tactical and speedy move-out thinking would be to have everything loaded into a designated vehicle bought just for that purpose, though I fully realize financial circumstances might prevent this. I have no good suggestions other than if you have a group, consider pooling funds to get the vehicles the group needs. One of the givens is that if each member or family is stocking up, each would need a vehicle to load the equipment into. One option is that one truck serves part of the group members, and as nonperishable stores are acquired, the designated truck for that group picks up the stores and parks at a designated member's residence. Good planning would have the fuel tank filled after every time the truck is used. A locking cap can be put on the fuel tank and the battery should be removed when parked to prevent theft. The cargo compartment should also be secured and even alarmed. During the acquiring of stores, no one outside of the group or individual should know anything about what is taking place. With money being short, the preparation process will take longer, and the individual or group member will have to balance purchases so all requirements are being equally attended to.

In a group, it will most likely be beneficial if specific members focus on certain supplies and the group holds periodic inventories. This is made easier if all members keep a running inventory. There are several ways this preparation may be accomplished, but I would suggest they be planned, organized, and constantly monitored by the group or individual. There should be nothing packed that is perishable. If

Multi-tools are a must in a survival situation.
(Dale C. Spartas/http://www.spartasphoto.com)

any time goes by and it spoils, all you will be doing is moving stores you cannot use.

When you have a little extra money, start looking at tools that will assist in the work you will have to do during survival times. Multi-tools, such as Gerber or Leatherman products, are a must. There will be many uses for small cutting blades, saws, pliers, and such, and to have them in one tool on your belt is a good thing. Take a look at the lists of what you will have to do. Let's take wood gathering for example. At the end of the skull session, you should have a list of equipment.

Wood Gathering

- Axe: how many?
- Hatchet: how many?
- Saw: how many and what type?
- Machete: how many?
- Sharpening stones and files: what type?
- Pry bars: what type and how many?
- Extra handles for axes and hatchets: how many?
- Maul or manual splitter: what type and how many?
- Transport cart: what type and how many?
- Tie-downs and come-a-longs: what type and how many?
- How many cords of wood will I need for warmth through the winter?
- How much wood will I need for cooking, washing, and cleaning?
- How and where do I store it?
- How do I keep it dry?
- Should I have a woodstove for heat and cooking?
- Can I cook and warm from the same fire pit?

Let's say this list is complete—do you see how quickly the load will grow? If you do this with the rest of the list, you will be amazed—and maybe a little intimidated—at how much work is in your future to ensure your survival. If you have a computer, the study of tools to assist you is only a finger touch away, or a visit to Home Depot or any logging supply store will answer all your questions. In a following chapter, I will provide websites that will assist you in your research and procuring the right equipment.

If the group is planning correctly, all equipment needs will be of equal importance. Money spent must give the group or individual full value and capability. It is sad but true, but in the procurement of equipment you get what you pay for. Saving money to get a piece of equipment that will not hold up under use and will break easily means you still wasted your money.

Take another look at what I just explained. You can spend money on cheap pieces of equipment, and they will last you a long time—if not used. I buy good equipment, so let's take my axes for example. I live in a rural state, but times are good and I am not in a survival situation. My axes have been in the garage unused for months, and they are lasting a long time. If I were in a survival situation and was cutting wood to prepare for winter, cooking, and cleaning, I might be using them daily or at least a few times a week. If they were not good steel with composite handles, they would not be around long and I would not be able to get good sustainable firewood without repairing them. Keep in mind the reason for this book is to Survive While Surviving. Woodcutting is a minimum of a two-man job if done correctly—one member cuts firewood while one member watches his back.

Also keep in mind, while doing anything in a survival situation where violence is possible, that no matter how good you are at securing yourself and conducting a tactical move, there are millions of people in the country who are trained by the military or playing paintball that are very good at sneaking up on someone or ambushing them while they are moving. Moving from paintballs to real bullets is an easy transition. For anyone reading this book with no training in what we are talking about who is worried, a good time-saver is finding an ex-military veteran who was in combat arms, another who was an engineer, and another who was a medic or doctor. That would be a good start to a group you would want to be in. But also keep in mind that all the good things we have available to us now mostly came to us in the last hundred and fifty years. We managed to survive brutal times, such as devastating winters and raiders or armies that were trying to kill us, for fifty or sixty thousand years with what we were carrying on our backs or had squirreled away wherever we were living or hiding. The problem is that no one living in the present knows how to survive under those conditions unless they are both trained and prepared. One more time: if you haven't started getting ready, start now. The clock is ticking.

It's easy for someone like me to say to pick a group or people for a group. I have talked with people who have asked how you pick the right people. In the preparation phase, this is usually difficult and time-consuming. If you are asked to join a group that is already preparing, that's easy. If you are looking for good people, spend time with them. If you have an initial feeling upon meeting them of dislike or mistrust, that feeling comes from within and is probably correct; they are not for your group.

If you feel good about them but during preparing or training they do not want to make the effort, they are not for your group. It's a given that people who will not be there for you when times are good will definitely not be there for you when times are bad. I am a combat veteran, and I would rather have no one guarding my back in a fight—at least I would know—than to have somebody back there who I am depending on but is not doing his job or has abandoned his position. That is a good way to be killed in some situations. Being alone is a good way to get killed in some situations, but at least you know the rules and can act accordingly.

Short-Term Disasters That Are Easy to Prepare For

- Major storms—hurricanes, tornados, etc.
- Floods
- Earthquakes
- Wildfires
- Major landslides
- Other major natural disasters

Any of these will be short-term as far as the resumption of emergency services is concerned. By this I am talking about police, fire, medical, and all the associated services we enjoy in this country. We always hear of people who do not have their houses repaired months after an event because their insurance claims are unpaid so they are still in shelters. But they have food, clothing, warmth in the cold, and all available reinstated emergency services. Based on historical facts in this country and around the world, I will say if you have a gun, ammunition, food, and water to keep you for a week, you will be okay.

This book is about having to do without services of any kind for a year or more. Some facts that most survival experts agree on are that if you have to survive a week or so, you need to be prepared as we have discussed. They also recommend getting a generator for light and, if you have warning of water being shut off, to fill your bathtub and any containers you have. This is all good advice and will make your life easier for a short period of time. If you are planning on leaving, you should still fill your bathtub in case you cannot get out. Also remember your water heater is full of water that will assist you in a survival situation. If the power is out, you should keep some cash for emergency buys, as ATMs will not be working. I also recommend keeping an emergency stash of any medications you may need, but in the end this is not really critical survival in my mind, as I have had times where I have been snowed in and trapped in my house for this amount of time.

The survival data I have read and some experiences I have had around the world verify that if for whatever reason you have to survive for a month with no services, you have severe problems that you do not have in the short term. One other thing, and I have been there many times, is that if you cannot turn on your tap and get water, you have some issues. If you have stored a supply of water for drinking, this is good. Hopefully you will have enough for sanitation purposes. If this is not the case, you may have to find water and then filter or purify it. In this case, a good filtration system is required. There are some good ones out there, and we will provide the websites later in this book. During this time, you will also need some tools to do things that will come up, and I believe basic carpentry tools will carry you through this time. You or family members may need basic medical attention. Most survival books recommend different emergency medical kits. This is good advice, but do not get a medical kit without the training to use it. If you have a generator, you should start rationing fuel right away. Fuel will be hard to come by a month into a total services shutdown. The upside of a generator is you have light when you need it. The downside is any light during a power outage is going to attract unwanted attention.

Do not go anywhere at this time without protection. Start thinking tactically and making tactical moves—at this time zombies will be prowling. I know people who own guns who say, "I don't think I could kill somebody." Believe me, nine out of ten of these types will.

All wars have conscientious objectors—most of them medics. I have seen this personally, and war stories are full of these gentle people. When caught in close combat where enemy troops overrun their position, they go bat shit crazy, pick up a fallen soldier's weapon, and become killing machines to protect themselves and their charges. It is a given that when people survive life-threatening situations, it changes their outlook on how life should be forever. If the situation goes long term—a month or more—especially if winter is in full swing, all services are cut off, and no fuel is available, the need for acquiring firewood will become paramount, most likely before the end of thirty days. If you have no means of heat, it will become critical immediately. Also, where are you going to burn it? A fire in the middle of your living room floor will quickly become a house-destroying fire. If you are on your game in preparing, you would have bought a kit and chimney pipes for a fifty-five-gallon drum that can quickly, with minimal carpentry skills, become a wood-burning stove.

I have sat in people's living rooms and talked about this and been asked by people sitting in a wooden house with a detached wooden garage, a wooden fence around the yard, and wooden furniture throughout the house, "Where am I going to get wood? We have no trees here." After I explain to them what wood is available, I generally hear, "I wouldn't have thought of that." With this in mind, do you think some training and preparation drills would be a good thing? Every tree that was cut down to build the local houses is still there, they are just in the shape of construction lumber, but this is still burnable, as soon after disaster many of those houses will be empty or abandoned. One of the benefits of tearing down these houses for firewood, besides keeping you warm, is it increases your ability to see farther and gives you better fields of fire in the event of an attack on your location. It will not be lost on other survivors that where there is smoke there is fire, and where there is fire there is warmth. You will attract many unwanted visitors.

It is easy for experienced people to forget where they come from. Fifty-plus years ago when I came into the army, I knew nothing about what I have already written in this book. Now fifty-plus years with a varied and sometimes exciting career behind me, I can write this book and try not to forget where I came from. To most civilians reading this book, they will be seeing this information for the first time. Even in this dangerous world, until 9/11 we lived in a fairly protected society. You only have to look at the terror and thousand-yard stares on the crowds running from the World Trade Center or the Pentagon after the planes hit to see how a disaster of epic proportions will affect the majority of our population. I will say during those events, a lot of civilians stood up and jumped in to help, and that will happen in any disaster. But take a look at the pathetic events in New Orleans after Katrina, and you see how unprepared our population is. It should not be lost on anyone that the government, which is supposed to have our backs, failed in quickly supporting some of our nation's singular national disasters. How well do you think they will do in a nationwide disaster?

If you have to survive from six months to somewhere past the year mark, total preparation must take place for you to have any chance of surviving. Things are going to start happening that you may not have thought of. During this time you will have been working hard, defending yourself and your supplies, and moving through littered streets or over rough terrain. In those six months, several things that will impact you, as well as the group you may have around you, will begin to take place.

Things to Prepare For

- Clothes will be worn out or starting to wear out and will have to be replaced or repaired.

- Shoes and boots will need to be replaced or repaired.

- If not maintained, weapons will begin to jam or break down.

- Tools will break and have to be fixed or replaced.

- Vehicles, if working, will have no fuel.

- Food and water supplies will be depleted.

- Hunting, fishing, and gathering will have to supplement your diet or become your diet.

- Major medical problems will present themselves.

- If in a winter area, warmth will become mandatory.

- Water purification will, as it always will be in a survival situation, become critical.

- Sanitation, both personal and in the living area, will become critical.

If groups or individuals do not prepare for these things prior to the event, they will never get accomplished to the level needed after disaster strikes. A big part of preparation is stashing barter material for

Events like those that took place in New Orleans after Hurricane Katrina reveal just how unprepared our population is when disaster strikes. (sandoclr, courtesy of iStock)

use when things get desperate. Bartering is always dangerous; it could be a trap and should be looked on as a tactical operation. Things that would be gold-like in a barter situation are food and water, of course, weapons or ammunition—never trade both at the same time—batteries, rope, wire, tie-downs, tools, and whatever people are requesting. I have stated before: never defend yourself and then leave the individuals' guns and ammunition behind. That also goes for equipment, clothes, and footwear. All are bartering or personal survival items. Going to barter should be rehearsed, considered an unknown situation that could go bad, and covered by other group members.

That may sound paranoid, but there are a lot of people in this country who cannot be trusted in good times, so they will not be better people in bad times. In this instance, if a group of armed people comes in to barter, the chance of a fight breaking out is diminished. If the barterers are bad people, they will wait for a group or individual they can handle. I also believe if they are bad the word will be out. A lot of barter societies consider the barter site neutral ground that benefits all, and that should be the main rule for starting a barter society. Barter societies have worked in places such as Bosnia, Somalia, Afghanistan, Russia, China, Rwanda, and many others around the world. They will work here if disaster strikes.

While preparing for disaster, many individuals and groups make unrealistic plans for moving to a survival location. I am comfortable with going to a remote location that will allow me to get there on a single tank of fuel, and I can do that where I live. I have friends who cannot do this, and I suspect there are many others planning to go to a place in the country. I have a friend who is looking at a seven-hundred-mile trip to his property of choice. With his current vehicles, he would have to refuel two or three times if he wanted a near-full tank when he arrived.

If he just loads his guns, ammunition, and tools he plans on taking, his vehicles will be full. No water, food, or other survival gear will fit. When I pointed this out to him, a kind of panic set in, and for the first time he started thinking properly on what he needed to do. I questioned him on the land he had bought at a good price—and it is a good piece of land with game on it, and it will be defendable with a little work. The biggest problem is that the nearest water source is two miles away and not on his property. This is no big deal, but once disaster strikes he is looking at a four-mile round trip to haul water at more than eight pounds a gallon. Currently there is no road to the water source. This is going to tie people up every day, summer or winter, and take away from other work that may be important to the survival of the group.

The bottom line is that he focused on some land he wanted but not enough on what he might require on it. When looking for land in a rural or remote setting, do not buy land that is going to increase what will already be a staggering workload just to survive. There are a lot of questions that come up about how to fund preparation. Families have to spend quality time together—it is what makes families strong and brings them happiness. One thing that can be done is to make preparation a family project and use the money that would be spent on certain outings to start procuring what you need. I will give you an example, and you can review what your family does. We have a four-year-old grandson, and in his mind he is a Ninja Turtle, as are millions of other four year olds. When the latest Ninja Turtle movie came out, he saw the previews on TV. From that minute on, it was a constant "We need to see this movie, when are we going?" We took him, my wife, and a couple other family members. At the end of the night, with movie, snacks, and parking, we spent one hundred and ten dollars. Had we waited for it to come out on DVD, we would have had that money to buy needed preparatory equipment. I suspect in every family's lives, savings like that are possible. I am not saying preparation is all you should focus on, but I know there is money being spent that could be better spent getting ready for your needs if disaster strikes. Once it does strike—and it's when, not if—the game is on, and you start with what you have.

Let's take a look at some good advice given in survival magazines for a long-term survival situation. One is to grow a garden as time goes by. This is good advice, and everybody nods their heads and collects and stores seeds to use when disaster strikes. I have heard no one ask valid questions that should be planned for during preparation—no matter if you live in a rural or urban area.

Good advice—grow a garden!

Questions to Consider During Planning

- Where do I plant it if I live in the city?
- Where do I plant it on my rural property?
- What do I need for tools?
- If water is scarce, where do I get it?
- How do I fertilize it?
- Once it starts to produce, how do I guard it?
- What materials need to be on hand to preserve vegetables for later meals?

I have seen good advice given in many survival venues but little on what growing a garden really means in a survival situation after disaster. For example, if you do not guard it, how do you stop people from stealing from it? If water is scarce, how do you have enough to keep the garden alive and producing? Let's take a look at reality and some things that will impact you once you plant a garden. Depending on where you live, the growing season will be at least two to three months and much longer in some parts of the country if weather cooperates and the garden is well tended. Where do I plant it in the city? The safest option would be that if your survival location is a building with a flat roof, plant it there. People do this as we speak with no issues. The problem of guarding it comes up if the roof can be readily accessed from adjoining buildings. If you do not guard it and people know of it, you will end up growing it for looters. Hiding it may not be an option on the roof if surrounding buildings are taller than the one you are occupying.

I think you see this problem clearly; you will have the same problem if you have a yard and plant it there. If it can be seen, hungry people will loot it. You also need to be as sure as you can that you will not be run out of your location by looters or raiders. It may sound funny to normal people, but planting a garden in a survival situation where looters and raiders are present places another tactical requirement on the group. Another issue is watering it if water is scarce, such as in a drought. Any pool of stagnant water that is not full of industrial waste can be used to water the garden, and with that being said, part of your preparation should have been the procuring of as many barrels as you can haul and sheets of plastic. If used properly, these barrels and plastic sheets will give you tons of extra water every time it rains. In tests in a perfect setting, a single day of moderate rain filled ten fifty-five-gallon barrels.

If we had more plastic sheeting and barrels, we could have filled as many as we wanted. In heavy rain, we would have more water than we wanted. This test was done in a state where it does not rain as much as it does in other states. Once the barrels are full, they need to be covered to prevent evaporation. I can tell you that if you are in a true survival situation, you will never have enough barrels and containers. Never let a rainstorm go by without washing yourself thoroughly. Take down the plastic sheeting after you stock up on water, as the sun and wind will eventually make it fall apart. Sheet metal roofs and downspouts on buildings can also be used to capture water. These are the types of questions that should be skulled by the group when deciding what to procure for the coming long-term disaster. I will also remind you to hang your plastic sheeting over barrels where you want the barrels to be. A fifty-five-gallon drum of water weighs four hundred and fifty-eight pounds, so you are not going to be able to move it easily.

During the preparation phase, there is the question of whether you will have to see at night. That answer is a resounding yes. First we need to look at batteries and what they will do for us. The survival manuals and schools say stock up on batteries, and this is, of course, good advice. I have packs of Duracell batteries that say they are guaranteed for ten years in storage. That certainly is a long enough time for us to come back from disaster. If we're not back, it will not matter. I have other data that says alkaline batteries are good for seven years in the package, so the time would be impacted by how long they were in storage before they were sold. Manufacturers say batteries are big business and they sell fast. There are good and bad flashlights out there, but all break or quit on you sooner or later. You will need several of all the kinds you determine you will need. All flashlights have information on how long a battery will last under heavy use, so it is a simple matter to determine what that time is and procure the amount of batteries you think you will need, as well as spare bulbs. Will this put you in possession of a truckful of batteries? It will if you can afford them. One thing I am certain of is that no matter how many you procure, you will eventually run out if the situation lasts long term. My recommendation for flashlights is any military- or industrial-grade light. I have used them every night during my career since they have been in existence. Lights are like everything else, you get what you pay for, but you will need to get what you can afford. There are also light sticks. These are in a package that you simply open and then bend the stick until you break a vial. The stick lights up to provide low- to high-intensity light for hours. They are of one-time use but provide good emergency light in several colors.

One thing to remember is that if violence is taking place in your area, lights also become the enemy. They give away your location and make you an easier target. You will be living in a parallel universe of survival needs and tactical requirements. Let's look at another question we should be skulling in our preparation phase.

Will I have to clean myself and the living area? Yes.

Necessary Equipment

- Soap: body and dish
- Hot water
- Toothpaste, brushes, mouthwash, toothpicks, and floss
- Bleach
- Bon Ami, Ajax, or similar cleaning powder
- Hydrogen peroxide

- Ammonia
- Vinegar
- Pine-Sol
- Baking soda
- Containers for carrying water and washing
- Rags and sponges
- Brushes, mops, and brooms
- Trash cans

This list can certainly be added to, but you are going to be operating in a survival situation. You will need as much as you can get, but this requires storage room and, if moving, room in the vehicles making the move. Failure to keep good cleaning habits will result in disease that could wipe out a city if it gets out of control. There is going to be a problem of contaminated water, especially in cities, which in itself will cause disease. An important part of cleaning is purifying water.

Failure to keep good sanitation standards will result in internal parasites, lung congestion, rashes, tooth decay, and many other sicknesses. Put those problems against a population that may be suffering from mild to critical malnutrition and dehydration and you have a recipe for disaster that will threaten all life in the area. Let's take a dose of reality and look at what is potentially a real scenario. Disaster strikes nationally, power is out, and most people are out of communication.

If you live in a large city, how many people in that city depend on life support provided by electricity? I do not know the answer to any particular city, but soon after disaster strikes, bodies are going to start piling up. Looting will start quickly in the majority of short-term disasters. I see no reason it will not start quickly in the situation we are talking about. This looting, as all looting does, will have violence attached to it, which will result in more bodies piling up.

A day or two into a long-term survival situation, there will be bodies that, if they are not removed, will attract rats and other animals and quickly become a disease threat. With emergency services disrupted and out of touch with the populace, who removes and burns or buries these bodies that have to be taken care of to prevent disease? We can only hope that the existing government establishes some semblance of order and concerned citizens step up and start taking care of this critical business. While taking care of this business, the people doing it will probably have to create a few more bodies by shooting some of the village idiots who will be trying to take what they have.

If you look at the studies of how much of the population will die if this event happens, we're in serious trouble. Just the thought of what may happen along these lines is reason to get out of town quickly. If you look at the Ebola problem in West Africa, there are reports from the capital of Liberia of bodies lying unattended in the streets. Things will get much worse if they are not attended to. This chapter on preparation is important in that it gets you to think, and that is the chapter's intent. Do not forget when reading this chapter that you will be living in a parallel universe. When answering the questions this chapter presents, think about what tactical requirements are raised by what you decide.

Let's try another question. Will I have to tell direction? Yes.

Necessary Equipment

- Maps
- Compass
- GPS
- Training in land navigation

As you forage and gather certain game and materials, you will have to go farther and farther from your survival location, and you may be forced to travel at night or under cloud cover. We live in the Northern Hemisphere, so if you can see the sun and know what time it is, you can roughly tell the cardinal directions of north, east, south, and west. You can do the same thing at night if you have clear skies and can see the Big Dipper and the North Star. If you are under cloud cover and have a GPS with working batteries, navigation is no problem. If you do not have GPS and have a cloud cover, a compass is mandatory to figure out cardinal directions and which way you should go. Those of you planning to head for the hills will find that losing direction in the dark in the middle of the woods is guaranteed. If you do not have a compass, you will never find the area you are looking for. Traveling most of the night in the wrong direction will put you miles off course.

To make sure you know what you are doing, a class on compass use would do you well. All Boy Scouts know how to use a compass, and so do many military veterans. When using a compass, you need to keep track of the direction you go when leaving your location, and that should be planned. Maps are handy, and you should have one. Learning to read a map is also strongly recommended. I have stated the redundancy in all survival data that holds true for learning how to read a map and compass. If disaster strikes, we are going to be sent back in time anywhere from one hundred years to the Stone Age. How well we have prepared and what survives the disaster will make the difference. But as we speak, we are in the age of total, instant information, and contact with schools and instructors is only a finger touch away. I will not waste time duplicating or plagiarizing data that is already at your fingertips. Now if you are lazy and won't do the work to learn, it would not matter if it were in this book because you wouldn't do the work from what you read here. You also will probably not survive anyway—few lazy people do in any critical situation.

When using a compass, you should travel with at least one traveling companion. This is because using a compass focuses a lot of your time on the compass; the same is true for maps and GPSs. When using any navigational aids in a survival or tactical situation, someone should be watching your back.

If you have gotten this far in the book, you now have many thoughts in your head, and that's good. I cannot tell you enough times how important it is to stay on your guard once disaster strikes. I have been in numerous combat situations, and I can tell you that you will fall into the trap that most humans do when on guard. The more time that goes by with nothing going on, the more you will get bored and lose focus. I can also tell you that people who want to do you harm can appear like magic inside your personal space and kill you before you can react. You must stay scared, as this will keep you alert. If days go by, not to mention weeks or months, with nothing serious happening, you will get sloppy. Down the road, someone will get to you. Group leaders are the answer here; tactical discipline must be ongoing and unrelenting. If the leaders themselves are weak, someone who isn't will kill the group. Trust me, I have done it in a couple of war zones to enemy troops who thought they were safe. Do not kid yourself, in a long-term survival situation, you will be in a war zone.

I would like to think that there will be large areas where the people pull together, help each other, and have some form of organization. That will probably happen, but while it does, these areas will be under constant threat from organized looters and raiders. If people reading this book think I am being too harsh, get on the Internet to see what went on during conflicts in Bosnia, the fighting in Somalia, and Rwanda. In our own country, look at hurricane Katrina, the Rodney King riots, or Ferguson, Missouri, after a white police officer shot and killed a black teenager. Looting and the burning of buildings took place in spite of a large police presence and a functioning government.

Within the smaller communities, the idea of pulling together is already mostly ingrained into people. They check on each other, and if someone has trouble, people are always there to help. I live in a community like that, which I am grateful for, and it is one of the reasons that I intend to stay here if disaster strikes. If things do go bad for whatever reason, I can get into a remote setting quickly. During the preparation part of getting ready, there are certain things that should become what the military calls standard operating procedures (SOPs). As a civilian, you can call them rules.

The Rules

- Everyone in the group knows what the group is doing.
- Do not talk about group business outside the group.
- All work and preparation protocol is equally distributed.
- Everyone takes designated training that is deemed necessary.
- If moving, all routes are physically checked.
- Every route has at least one checked alternate route.
- All vehicle fuel tanks making the move are kept full.
- Critical items are not all put in the same vehicle.
- Meet on a group-determined schedule to plan and check inventories.
- The meeting and who runs it should be rotated through the group.

- Any group member who becomes detrimental to the group is dealt with quickly.
- Plan for all plans to fail if the right situation is present, and have backup plans.

This list is to give you ideas and a good start. Depending on your situation and place of residence, you may want to add to it. Within all groups and communities who are getting ready for disaster, there are many good ideas, and everyone needs a chance to provide their input. By doing this, groups reduce the always-present chance of running with a bad idea and wasting time and money. In saying that, when checking planned alternate routes, you might find that you cannot use it for whatever reason. That's not wasted time or money—that's something you need to know before you stake your life or the lives of the group on it.

The best use of time needs to be looked at constantly. If CPR training or range training is going to take place in the morning, that afternoon would be ideal for a group planning meeting. Save time and get more accomplished anytime you can. One thing that ensures the success of the group is the monitoring of all group members. If a group member is not completing his or her given responsibilities or is missing meetings and training, they are part of the problem, not the solution, and get rid of them quickly. That individual will not improve when things go bad. I have talked a little about this in different chapters, and I am serious as death on this subject. If a member is not 100 percent dedicated to saving the group's lives, he or she is not needed by the group.

If it is a family group, this decision will be the most difficult, but any way it goes, the family must make the ultimate decision. Any decision made in family groups will cause some hard feelings. The only thing I will say here is that if a bad decision is made at the family level, that will not be a first. If it destroys the family continuity and the family dies because of it, that will not be a first either. People will say, "Man, this guy is over the edge." If disaster has struck and we are all over the edge, we are going to have to make many unwanted decisions. These decisions should always be made to benefit the many.

I do not expect the millions of people who have not been in life-threatening or life-altering experiences to understand this, but everyone has the survival gene in them to one degree or another.

I also think that, like conscientious objectors previously discussed, most will make the right decisions. At any length, I have no stake in these families or groups, so I can only wish you luck and Godspeed in making the right decisions.

With the above being said, let's go back to group preparations. We talked about the actual traveling to your rural site by the routes you have chosen. I have friends that must initially travel on interstates to get in close proximity to their chosen sites, and unless we have a major flood, earthquake, or some disaster that closes these roads, they will most likely be open. If we lose the power grid and riots break out in cities along the primary route, we can divert to our secondary route if we received news of this over our survival radios. This is where most people make a serious mistake by not actually going to their rural site by driving this route. If something happens to close both your primary and secondary routes of travel, you may have to start your survival career in a place not of your choosing.

If this should happen, there are several options available to you. One is to start survival operations where you are and monitor your survival radio for information that the routes are open. Be prepared for that not to happen. If you are blocked by circumstances, a group plan and action meeting needs to take place, but remember you are now in a survival and tactical situation. The gist of this meeting should be whether, based on the route you have taken, this is the best place to start out or if there was a place along the route that would be better. For instance, if you are in an area of little vegetation and no observable water but you have an area behind you with forests and a river, this move is a no-brainer. Once you make the move back to the better area, an onboard fuel check needs to be made to determine how far you can get from this point if circumstances force a move.

At this point maps should come out and at least two plans should be put in place in the event of another forced move. We have talked about the following statement previously in this book. Know where you are going, how you are geting there, and what equipment you need. Once settled, a good move would be to find out if you are on state or federal land. This would be good, as when disaster on a national level hits there is basically no state or federal anything taking place. If it's private property, try to find the owner—or he or she may find you—and work a deal with them along the lines of, "If you give us permission to stay here and you need help, we will give it to you." They would be foolish to not take that deal, but in the case that they don't, you should have two plans to facilitate your next move.

I am told by people who have read this book that what I am saying is valid, but I am expecting normal people to put in a huge effort to accomplish what we are talking about. I'm telling you what will happen if disaster strikes and what you need to do to have a chance of surviving. My job is to write this book, but what you do with the information in it is your call. In the end I am confident that people who think it might happen will start preparing. The rest get what they get.

The lists in this book are solely to assist your planning, but how much funding you have to put into it will mean you have either a quick or slow road ahead of you. If you have a group that is thinking alike, serious in their intent, and is comprised of people of varying economic means, the wealthier members should put in a little extra when they can to make this happen. The stronger and more prepared the group is, the better their chance of survival. The wealthier group members putting in a little extra will make the group stronger. I am sure people naturally understand this, and whatever extra any group member puts in will pay dividends starting the second disaster strikes.

I have looked at a few people's preparation efforts, and most were on the right track. I have seen a few things that could have been handled better. One of these is ammunition storage or the lack of. I have talked with people who have ammunition in open containers, rounds taken out of the manufacturer's wrapping, and the bullets dumped into open boxes. I am told they will be easier to get in the middle of a fight. If you are in a fight where quick reload ammunition needs to be on hand, one or more of these three things are happening:

- You have made no plans nor taken training in what to do here.
- You have only one magazine for your weapon or no speed loaders.
- You are alone and in trouble.

I am going to throw a word out here: corrosion. Look it up. Dirty or corroded ammunition will jam or damage your guns. First, leave all ammunition in factory packaging until ready to load it into magazines or guns. Second, if you get military ammunition cans to put your ammunition into, leave it in the factory boxes and put those into the military cans. Third, store the ammunition in a cool dry place. If you cache it, use self-sealing boxes that are made to keep food fresh. Keep the ammunition in the factory boxes when placing it in the food storage containers, and add a small desiccant bag in each food storage box. The cache should be located in as dry a place as possible. Although the food boxes are waterproof, I always spray the seal line with bed liner or plastic sealant. Square PVC tubing that can be capped on each end has also been a winner for me. People living in different locations need to experiment to see what works for them. A good reference found easily on the Internet is a book by my old friend Ragnar Benson called *Modern Weapons Caching.*

How do we get by without an emergency grab for ammunition to reload our guns with? Combat reloads are important, and training and practice will make you proficient at it. This is my take on how to not have to emergency reload. I have at least ten magazines on my survival belt. I have different automatic pistols on three survival belts, and they all have ten magazines on them. My assault rifle has ten magazines on my combat harness.

Our group training revolves around the scenario that we are in a fight at our survival location and designated shooters have a loader that reloads every magazine ejected by the shooter. We are also not clairvoyant, so if we are attacked by a zombie horde everyone will be shooting, and we will see who is around at the end of the fight. Where I live that will not happen, but if there is a chance it will happen where you live, I suggest you get a couple of machine guns. I am not being facetious here; it is going to get rough, and you need to get as ready as you can. That's all any of us can do. We will not know where the trip will take us if disaster strikes until we get there. If outside the survival location, never eject an empty magazine and leave it where it fell. Most combat-experienced guys have a dump bag on their gear or a cargo pocket where used magazines go. If you eject them and leave them, you will soon run out. As a side note, when you clean your gun, clean your magazines.

All long guns should have slings. Get one- or three-point slings so your long gun is attached to you. That way, if you fall down in the dark or have to use both hands, you don't have to worry about your gun. Someone should always be watching your back. With this said, will you ever be alone? The answer is yes. I learned as a young soldier about how quickly you can be had. We were on a training exercise and had been told our weapon was to never leave our hands or reach. I was out of water, and we were by a stream. I walked about ten meters from our perimeter and leaned my rifle up against a tree within reach per instructions. I pulled out my canteen and filled it from the stream. The total time was probably less than thirty seconds, but when I turned around to get my rifle, my squad leader was standing there with my gun in hand. I never heard him come up and take my rifle. His question stayed with me for the rest of my career and until this day. "What if I was an enemy soldier, asshole?" I have generally stayed an asshole until this day, but I have never forgotten that lesson.

People can get inside your personal space and kill you in seconds. Heed my ramblings in this book, as your life and the group's lives may depend on it in a survival situation. Sooner or later as you acquire stores for your survival, you will max out your storage or vehicle capacity. This will take place whether you are staying in your house, a group member's house, or making a move to a rural location. At this time, you will need to determine what stores are critical and lifesaving and what stores are nice to have. Make the critical lifesaving stores take priority.

Let's talk about the vehicles, their loads, and how much we put on each truck. It is important to cross-load and not put all the critical items on one truck. We want to make the best use of the space we have, especially on vehicles. In a perfect world, everything packed in the vehicle is in square packaging that can be stacked with no loss in storage space. I can almost assure you that will not happen, but you can get close. Now let's talk about the tactical part of the move. When moving trucks, from pickups to ten tonners, through areas where you may be attacked, good tactical protocols are as follows:

One shooter is in the passenger seat, where he or she can shoot out of the window while the vehicle is moving. Four shooters are in the pickup bed and have the front, right, left, and rear of the truck covered if the vehicle is attacked.

However, this is most likely not going to happen. Trucks will probably be almost, if not completely, overloaded with stores. This is not tactically sound, although undoubtedly realistic, but there are ways to get around this depending on how large the group is. During preparation before disaster strikes, I assume most of the group owns their own vehicles. Some probably come from a two-vehicle household, so not counting trucks owned for the move, the group has several vehicles. Here is where group size is important. If the tactical recommendation above cannot happen because of group size or lack of vehicles, a group vehicle with at least three shooters should be in front and in back of each truck carrying stores. If this is not possible, the group needs to determine if they have enough vehicles and people to safely make the move. We are never going to agree on group size when getting ready for disaster and surviving for any length of time, as all of us are set in our ways due to our life experiences. The best advice I can offer here is that two heads are better than one, and well-thought-out group decisions will usually be the right one. This does not mean unforeseen circumstances will not interfere once disaster happens.

Revisit what I have already written about what makes a functional group. There must be enough people in the group to ensure the work can be done to Survive While Surviving without exhausting everyone in it and making the group ineffective. I can make recommendations based on experience, but I also know circumstances may force less than desirable actions. Groups are on their own here, as they will be when disaster strikes. In the situations we are talking about, bigger groups are better, and more jobs to benefit the group can be accomplished. In saying this, I realize that bigger groups require more food and water, as well as other resources. I would still like to have a group and take my chances with one that has enough people to secure it and its location. There will never be a perfect situation once disaster strikes, but well-put-together groups will have less inner-group friction. Groups will have strong, well-balanced group members, and they will have weaker members with a tendency to overreact in some cases and underreact in others. Leadership is the answer, as it always is in critical situations.

You have read the following before in this book and probably in other books you have acquired. Good leadership does not mean bad things are not going to happen, it just means that the chances of dealing with them and surviving the encounter are raised in the group's favor.

Chapter Six

Individual Protective Equipment

Historical references are full of lone individuals and groups of people surviving under terrible life-threatening conditions. Mountain men are famous for disappearing into remote areas and making it with what they had on their backs or pack animals. They made it with equipment that was the most modern available at the time. How did they survive without what we have today? That's simple—it didn't exist—but they also had to Survive While Surviving. Can we survive without neat equipment that is available to us today? Sure we can—the mountain men proved that—but why should we if we do not have to? The equipment that currently exists will make our survival more ensured.

In previous chapters, I included lists to get you to think about what you might need to survive. In this chapter, we will cover some of the equipment that is available in these modern times. I am not associated with any company or manufacturer and have no dog in this fight. Because it is in this book does not mean I am recommending that specific brand. As in all situations in life, you will have to make your own decisions.

We will first discuss weapons and ammunition. If a critical national event happens, you will have to protect yourself during everything you do after. You will have to Survive While Surviving. Some of the equipment listed in this chapter is expensive, and I understand that budgets will ultimately determine what an individual can acquire. Like everything else in all disaster and survival thinking and decision-making, hard decisions will be the order of the day. Although there is not much order to this book, I will try to establish some here by following the list of individual protective gear in Chapter One.

Shotguns

Shotguns are excellent close protection weapons and are recommended for personal and home defense. They are short-range weapons used worldwide with devastating effects; the best ammunition for self-defense is buck shot or slugs. For hunting use, there are bird shot and small game loads. There are shotguns with pistol grips that make the weapon shorter, but if you are going to use yours for hunting, get one with a full stock and hunting sights. Shotguns are perfect for in-house defense. Almost every police and military unit worldwide uses them. They are one of the best weapons for fighting inside structures and for short ranges, such as under one hundred yards outside.

M4s or Assault-Type Weapons

These are typically calibers of .223/5.56, .308/7.62 rifle rounds. There also are knock-offs in 9mm and 10mm, but those are like shooting a pistol bullet out of a rifle—not that it won't kill someone, but you lose a lot of range and power that a rifle bullet provides. AK47s come under the heading of assault rifles, as do numerous other weapons. Assault rifles come with ten-, twenty-, or thirty-round magazines. Higher capacity magazines are available, but I find them hard to carry. You will have to make your own decision. These weapons require training from professionals, as do all weapons. When you type in "assault weapons," your search engine will give you all the information you need.

Another good search would be manufacturers of assault weapons. You will also find many accessories for the M4 and other assault rifles. Many great sights and gun lights are available from numerous manufacturers. I am a fan of gun lights, but many of the sights available take batteries. Sooner or later, if the situation goes long term, you will run out of batteries. A good setup for rifles and assault weapons is a scope and iron sights on the weapon. This is my personal choice, but check out all options and make your own decisions.

Note: All long guns need slings, and all weapons need cleaning gear to maintain. Leave ammunition in the factory packaging until ready to load into magazines or weapons. Have extra parts, as weapons will break or eventually wear out.

Hunting Rifles

These come in all sizes and calibers for the untrained. You military guys and other shooters really do not have to read this chapter. Use .308 or a similar caliber, learn to shoot, get comfortable with guns, and see where you want to go. Put a scope on all long guns. There are a lot of battery-powered sights out there that are good, but in the situation we are talking about, save batteries for flashlights, as they are going to get hard to find. Get professional training. As with the assault weapons above, you must make the choice that's best for you. I am set in my ways and stick to what I know best, but that does not necessarily mean you have to agree.

.22 Rifles and Pistols

For those of you who are untrained, these guns fire only .22 caliber ammunition. The pistols come as revolvers or automatics. They are great for small game, although you can kill a deer with them and use them for defense. They are excellent in a survival situation, especially for the individual survivor, because the ammunition is small and light so you can carry a lot of it. If you go with a rifle and pistol, both should take the same ammunition. These guns are accurate and easy to shoot. Most kids learning to shoot start out with .22 caliber weapons. As this

Hunting rifles come in all sizes and calibers for the untrained. Make the choice that's best for you. (Dale C. Spartas/http://www.spartasphoto.com)

book is being written, there is a shortage of .22 ammunition in some areas of the country, and I am told in certain areas you can only buy two boxes at a time. If that's the case, that's the way you buy it. There are always ways to get any ammunition you require.

Combat Pistols

There are numerous revolvers and automatic pistols available. I am going to tell you to go the automatic pistol route in 9mm, 10mm, .40 caliber, or .45. There are a lot of good pistol guys out there with good advice, so listen to them if you run into them and then make your own decisions. All pistols need a holster for carry and cleaning gear for maintenance. In a perfect world, the group should all have the same pistols so magazines and ammunition are the same. When you clean your pistol, clean the magazines at the same time. Revolvers are simpler and require less maintenance. I do not use them for a combat pistol—it's an Army thing.

Note: It is good policy that if you have a weapon that takes magazines to use magazines made by the same company that made the gun. There are a lot of excellent aftermarket magazines available, so talk to your instructors and make your own decision.

Binoculars and Flashlights

There are so many binoculars, flashlights, and other optical and lighting systems out there. A book much larger than this one could be written and not cover all of them. They range in price from a few dollars to many hundreds of dollars. Get what you can afford, but remember that you get what you pay for. For flashlights or anything with a battery, get as many as you can. With both flashlights and binoculars, do not throw them around or use them as impact weapons, as that will shorten their life. In my career, binoculars and flashlights were used as much as, if not more than, any other piece of equipment in the field. Carry both in protective pouches.

Knives

There are literally millions of them out there. For the situations we are discussing in this book, I say each individual needs two good fixed-blade knives with blades from six to eight inches, a sheath for carrying them, and a good folding knife with about a four-inch blade. Prices vary and so does durability and edge holding capability. I personally carry one double-edged knife as one of the two fixed blades. I also suggest you take some defensive and offensive knife training. I will catch hell here from the safety guys, but when training, use real knives. Training with rubber knives gives you confidence that falls apart once facing a real knife. This is my take on it. Is there a chance you can be injured? Yes. If you are injured and have stitches or deep cuts, do not quit training or look for sympathy—once disaster happens, you are going into a situation where every round will be a championship round, and you will not be able to lose without losing your life. Train real or pay the price.

Note: When shopping for knives, if you pick it up and it doesn't feel right, that's not your knife. It's supposed to feel like it is part of your hand.

Machetes

There are many tools like machetes that are called bush knives, as they are used for clearing brush, that are a good tool to have. Buy what you can afford. The better the metal they are made of and the stronger the handle, the longer they will last. They should not be used for breaking rocks, cutting barbed wire fences, or felling large trees. They also do not cut metal telephone poles. You can purchase them in most hardware or sporting goods stores. They are also great defensive and offensive weapons should the need arise.

The better the metal the machetes are made of and the stronger the handle, the longer they will last. (Predrag Vuckovic, courtesy of iStock)

Combat Harness

A combat harness is what carries your fighting gear. There are many models. You need one that is comfortable to wear—good luck—that will carry your ammunition, knife, and the self-defense gear you will need to secure yourself day to day. Every group member needs one. In your search engine, type in "manufacturers of combat harnesses" to see what is available. Do not order one through the mail; you need to try it on before you buy one—your life depends on it.

Utility Belt

This is a heavy-duty belt that you would use to carry a few magazines and maybe a knife, flashlight, tool, and the things you might want if you ran into trouble and did not have your combat harness. You would also wear it daily just in case. Try them on before you buy them, as you want as much comfort as you can get.

Rucksack

There are many hundreds of makes and models. Stay away from the school kid backpack and lean toward military or extreme weather gear. They are going to get hard use, and if not of very good quality, it will wear out quickly. Also, bigger is better, as you will live out of them, especially in a rural area. This does not mean you should not have smaller packs for different work. Packs should fit well and be comfortable—one size or type does not fit all. Packs that are not comfortable when empty or with little weight will be painful when fully loaded and carried for any length of time. Sporting goods shops sell them.

Pellet Guns

I left these out of the real gun list, but these guns are great and almost silent small game hunters. Do the research and buy a good pellet gun, along with a couple thousand pellets. You can spend less than a hundred dollars and have a lifetime of small game rounds. Make sure it has good sights on it and that you get it zeroed. My pellet guns have a velocity of 1250 feet per second. Another option is pellet pistols, and they will also work well on small game. Using pellet guns for small game saves real bullets for protecting yourself and your survival location. If you get really desperate, you could use pellets to reload your shotgun rounds if you have that capability. Draw a life-sized likeness of a rabbit or a duck on cardboard and practice until you get really good with the gun. You should also consider getting range help if you need it.

Note: Bear, deer, and elk are <u>NOT</u> small game. Rabbits, squirrels, rats, cats, and birds are small game—use pellets.

Pellets are ammunition, so do not waste them. Use pellets on small game instead of using your ammunition for your hunting rifles and M4-type weapons—those are for large game and self-protection. Pellets and .22 caliber ammunition are for small game, although on any day you can kill a deer and protect yourself with a .22.

Canteens and Hydro-Packs

When talking about hydration in a critical situation, I prefer canteens since they are more durable than hydro-packs. I have carried the same canteens for many, many years. In that time, I have seen dozens of hydro-packs on my buddies that have sprung leaks or had valve problems. There are many people who will disagree with me, and that is okay. You have to make your own decisions. Whatever you purchase, go the military route, as they are made for extreme circumstances like what you will be in. Keep in mind that my suggestions have worked for me, but there are a lot of people out there who are smarter and have more experience, so listen to all instructors and make your own decisions based on training and experience.

Clothes

If we are faced with a long-term disaster, you will need the toughest clothes made. Work clothes and extreme weather clothes would fit the bill. Repair materials for the clothes you have will be needed. You are going to be in hard times, and your clothes will be either destroyed or fall apart over time. Check work clothes stores or farm supply stores for the toughest over-the-counter clothes. If you find a body with better clothes than you, this will be a good deal. If they do not fit you, they may fit another group member or be great barter material down the road.

Boots

There is no good news here for thin budgets, as you will have to spend money to get good boots. You will need at least two pairs, but more would be better for long-term survival. Do not throw away your current running shoes or boots that you bought at the local everything store, as you will need them when in the survival location. If you know police or soldiers, use them as a resource for good boots. In my experience, they will give you good information. The one thing that will happen in a survival situation is that everyone is going to become somewhat of an infantryman or -woman. One of your most valuable assets will be your feet—leave no stone unturned in taking care of them.

Helmet

Any impact-resistant helmet will do: military, motorcycle, bike, etc. I guarantee if you are hit in the head during your survival travels by a thrown rock or metal pipe, your first—or last—thought will be, *I sure wish I had a helmet on.* Go get a good impact helmet. Every group member needs one. Head injuries are one of the most debilitating complications when living in a time of little to no medical care available. Every effort needs to be made to protect your vital areas from injury, whether man-caused or accidental. I hate helmets, but I wear them when working or in combat situations.

Body Armor

Again, there is no good news for thin budgets. Body armor is expensive, and I do not expect you to run out and get some, as you have a lot more pressing things you need. There is body armor that will stop rifle rounds and pistol rounds; others will stop only pistol rounds. It is good to have and saves lives. Rifle-bullet-stopping body armor is recommended. It is also protective equipment that may be the difference between living or dying.

Eye Protection

All professionals who go to work with guns wear eye protection. There are a lot of options available, and some of them are very expensive. Is it really needed? For those of you who have not been in a gunfight in a building or in a building getting shot at from outside, here is some insider information: fragments, both high and low velocity, in the form of glass, masonry, wood, and bullet jackets fly around. If hit in the eye with even a low-velocity fragment, at the least you have major troubles and at the worst you are blind. I highly recommend getting eye protection. Any sporting goods store will have these, as well as workplace safety stores. Some of the tactical eye protectors are expensive. There are companies that make tactical eye protection, and these are easily found on the Internet.

Knee and Elbow Pads

If you are one of the unlucky ones who, for whatever reason, has to stay in an urban environment and do what you may have to do in a survival situation, knee and elbow pads will become your best friend. I had to get a new knee because I was not wearing knee pads when I should have been. After the disaster, I am sure there will be no more knee surgeries as important items run out, such as painkillers. Any sporting goods store or military surplus store will have what you need.

Extendable Baton

Most police officers carry these devices on duty. For the situations we are talking about in this book, they would be excellent for every group member to have. They are an impact weapon that can be used when assisting another group member, when you do not have to use a bullet, or it's all you have when attacked. They can be carried on a belt anytime you are awake and moving, and once pulled, a flick of the wrist gives you a defensive baton. Like all other weapons, batons take training and practice. If you purchase a baton, be sure to include a carrying sheath.

OC Spray

OC is commonly called pepper spray and is used by both police and civilians for self-defense. The younger group members who may not be effective in a physical confrontation can incapacitate even the biggest looter or raider with OC. It is sold over the counter in many states. Like any other weapon, you need to get training and then practice. OC can be carried in your pocket or a carrier on your belt. I have used it many times in my career, and it has worked on everyone I used it on except one individual, who appeared to be immune. I have heard many stories over the years of others it did not work on, but I still consider it one of the best nonlethal defensive weapons.

Hatchet or Tomahawk

These are great defensive or offensive weapons that deliver devastating wounds and kinetic energy. Carried on either a belt or combat harness, they give the group member another option besides using ammunition.

Like knives, they should not be brought to a gunfight, but there is a place for them in critical events. Like all other weapons, they take training and practice. Tomahawks are weapons and should not be used as a hatchet. You will find them in most sporting goods stores.

Bows: Recurve, Compound, and Crossbow

Bows and arrows have been around thousands of years and are still used today, but they are better than ever. For Surviving While Surviving, they are the ultimate silent hunter. You can take down an elk with a hunting arrow, and you can use them for self-defense. All sporting goods stores have these great devices. If you purchase a bow, be sure to get practice arrows along with hunting arrows, as a bow requires practice. Keep in mind that whether you have a standard bow or a crossbow, you will need a quiver to carry extra arrows. Learning to make your own bow and arrows is also a good skill to have in a survival situation.

Personal Medical Kit

Everyone should have a personal medical kit with dressings for wounds, tourniquets, clotting bandages, etc. The initial first aid for trauma wounds is important and generally lifesaving. The group should have a large medical kit with surgical implements and trained personnel to use it. Unfortunately, in the situation we are talking about, serious injuries requiring surgery will in most cases result in death. If there is a group member with any medical knowledge, he or she should continue advanced medical training until disaster strikes. Group members with medical training should also be the ones to procure the group's medical equipment.

This covers my recommendations for a group of people who may or may not know much about this equipment. There are numerous manufacturers for each item on this list, so I suggest you do some online research prior to making any purchases. Do your research as if your life depends on it!

I know those who are prepared and working on their survival equipment or are soldiers, police, or outdoorsmen will ask why I went to the trouble to explain what everybody knows. Those from our community know this information, but there are countless millions out there that do not have a clue. In the group that knows nothing about this equipment, I am sure many will say, "Crap, this is going to be a long haul—almost impossible." My answer to them is good thinking—you are right. If you're in the group that feels you need to start preparing for a major disaster, go back and read the introduction to this book and get to work.

If you are living in a rural or urban setting, reread the appropriate chapter and take the lists in this book and get to work. I cannot help you; only you and your group can do that. The best anyone can tell you is that disaster is probably going to strike between now and the end of your life. You either have to roll the dice and hope it does not happen, or if you know you do not gamble well, get busy and start preparing. Look at your family or yourself in the mirror and ask what you are going to do if people start breaking into your house to get what is in your pantry. After that self-analysis, look in your pantry and ask yourself if you are ready for disaster.

This chapter is on individual protective gear. If each individual in the group has this gear, then you have also got group protective gear. Depending on the size of the group, you should be able to defend the survival location and any gathering party that goes outside the survival location looking for food, water, and needed equipment. This does not mean you will not experience casualties that will weaken the group over time. Keep in mind that you are probably a well-trained and equipped group among many prowling the area.

Our country is no different than any other modern country in that we depend almost daily—and sometimes several times daily—on a supply of food and critical items being delivered to us. For those of you who have no idea what happens on a daily basis, spend some time on a street where there is a pharmacy or major grocery store and count how many Fed-Ex, UPS, and eighteen-wheel trucks unload packages at the loading docks. If you live in an area where the next hurricane or major weather event is predicted, look at how fast shelves in these stores are depleted. We live in a fragile society, and panic, quickly followed by violence, will happen if things go bad. The longer they go bad, the worse it will get. Yes, stores will be the first to be looted, and that will happen quickly. Houses will be next.

What you read in these pages is to get you to think. Some will start what should be lifelong work to prepare to survive a disaster—or at least raise the chances considerably of surviving. However, it will all be for nothing without the mental fortitude to do what you may have to do. Keep in mind that what we have learned in the warrior community in this country, and indeed the world, since the beginning of human combat is that good intentions do not make mental fortitude. Neither do they get you ready for diversity and combat. What gets you ready is disciplined training where you sweat, sometimes bleed, and hurt to your heart while still heading where you have to go to successfully complete the task. Can I tell you that you can do it an easier way or that equipment is more important than people with the right mental attitude? The answer is NO. Get to work!

Now let's talk about personal gear and how you use it. Warriors, commandos, and guys with the equipment already, this is not for you. I will start out simple so you understand the hows and whys of why we have to do what we do.

- Survival is a full-time everyday job.
- Tactical living is a full-time everyday job.
- You are going to have to Survive While Surviving every day.

In this chapter, I have provided a list of an enormous amount of equipment to ensure your survival or that of your family or group. Are you going to carry all of it everywhere you go? Of course not. If you could, you would probably not need any gear at all.

Let's review the weapons I recommended: rifles or long guns, hunting rifles, M4s or assault rifles, and combat pistols. Because of their short range, shotguns are not rifles, but we will include them here. It's important that you know how to use the different guns that you should have available as a member of the survival location guards or the gathering party. As in everything we do with guns, you must pay strict attention to ammunition management. Do not just shoot to feel good or scare people; that's ammunition you will need later to save lives and protect the group. Good training will teach this.

Defending the Survival Location

If you need to defend the survival location, depending on approaches into the site and where you perceive that you need to defend yourself, there may be ranges from across the room to several hundred yards involved in your self-defense and that of the survival location. Your choices would be the M4 or hunting rifle with scope, shotgun, and pistol. Where would you use each of these? When observing out of windows, use the hunting rifle first because of its range and accuracy. Use the M4 if you do not have a hunting rifle. Do not waste ammunition once a looter is down; do not shoot again unless he or she becomes a threat.

Use shotguns and pistols for any close-range shooting inside the survival location or in close proximity to doors and windows. Shotguns are excellent for engaging looters coming through doors or

It's important that you know how to use the different guns that you should have available in a survival situation. (Dale C. Spartas/http://www.spartasphoto.com)

windows. If fighting inside the survival location and you run out of ammunition in your rifle or shotgun, transition to your pistol. Practice this in training.

As discussed above, batons, OC, and hatchets are good defensive weapons. While guarding the survival location, having a utility belt on with these items would be a good idea. If you decide you have to go outside the survival location, put on your combat harness with its extra magazines and equipment. If you do not know what you are going to be facing, be as prepared as possible when leaving the survival location.

The defense of the survival location, especially in the early days of surviving, will be critical. If you have well-stocked shelves and rooms, the last thing you will want to do is lose them. In the early days when you are well stocked, there will not be as much of a need for gathering parties as there will be once time goes by. You should start rationing as soon as disaster hits. If it all goes well, things may be straightened out in a month or so, but do not count on it. Even with well-stocked shelves, if you can fish or hunt, do so. Smoke the meat and fish to preserve it and add to your stock.

When defending the survival location, your personal protective gear does not all have to be worn. The survival location should be

Keep rucksacks handy in case there's a need to leave the location quickly. (warren-goldswain, courtesy of iStock)

prepared so extra ammunition and defensive gear is in the places that will support the defense. For instance, if you have fortified the corners, a shotgun with extra ammunition should be there. Anything for reloading or defense of the location should be in place. Rucksacks and any other gear that defenders would want to take with them in the event that they would have to leave the location quickly should be located where each member can pick it up, put it on, and go do what they have to do.

If you think I have a hang-up on guns, in the situations we are talking about, I do. It's going to get rough if disaster strikes. I know preppers who have many times more guns and ammunition than I have recommended here. This chapter is for the ones who are just starting to prepare and for the ones who are preparing and may not have thought about what it's really going to take to Survive While Surviving.

Defending the Gathering Party

When out with the gathering party, the chance of being fired on from a close-range location is good. There will be as many or more times that you will have to shoot at longer ranges. The gathering party should have a mix of hunting rifles and M4s or similar weapons, and everyone should have a pistol. These are the primary weapons I would recommend for travel outside the survival location. If the intent of the gathering party is hunting small game, certain party members should have pellet guns and .22s as secondary weapons. Never get into a gunfight with a pellet gun! If going after big game, bows and arrows should be carried for silent hunting. Everyone should be in their combat harness, rucksack, body armor, helmet, knee and elbow pads, and eye protection, especially in an urban environment. Rucksacks should have a medical kit, extra ammunition, water, and whatever else members think they will need. To the untrained, you will find the daily grind of carrying needed gear tiring and even painful at times, but you will be doing what every combat soldier has done since there were armies and wars.

If it's winter, extra warm clothes should be carried by all if there is a chance that the party will be out overnight. Half the party should carry sleeping bags. The reason only half carry sleeping bags is that in bad areas half should be on guard while half of the party sleeps. This can be modified if the group is in a good defendable location. Forgetting your tactical responsibilities will sooner or later get you killed. If using vehicles, there should be a minimum of two in a perfect world. If having to use pushcarts, no more than half the gathering party should have them, as the other half are on movement security. These actions are taken if there is a complete breakdown of society and looter and raider groups are out looking for an opportunity to score a successful raid. As time goes by, this would be a constant threat, especially in an urban environment.

What Could Possibly Go Wrong?

- The defenders of the survival location may be driven out of the location while the entire group is in it.

- The defenders may be driven out while gathering parties are gone.

- The gathering party may be ambushed and not return.

- The gathering party may be trapped by looters and cannot return.

- The gathering party returns with casualties and no food or water.

- One of the gathering parties returns and reports the other gathering party is trapped by looters at a known location.

I think these six bullet points cover enough to get people thinking. What started as a normal day can quickly turn into a disaster that will have a severe impact on the group no matter what its size is. Let's take them one at a time.

Basic Decisions That Will Have to Be Made

- If the group is driven out of the survival location, it will mean either they were forced out or decided to leave because of circumstances. If forced out, they are probably under attack and are going to have to make a tactical evacuation—possibly under fire. This would tax a well-trained military unit. At a group level, this should have been planned and rehearsed. Compounding the evacuation, there may be group casualties. This is where group size matters—too small and you are probably dead. A large group could evacuate wounded and head to the rally point while covered by the rest of the group. If the survival location is surrounded by a large group of looters, a breakout is going to be costly. In this instance surrender is not an option. No good news here.

- If driven out while gathering parties are gone, all protocols in the first scenario are in play, plus the group is now split. If there are no communications possible with the gathering party, there should be a plan to meet at the rally point. This plan would prevent the gathering party from returning to the survival location and being ambushed by the group that forced the evacuation. All gathering parties should return to the survival location by way of the rally point, especially if there is no communication available between the survival location and the gathering party. This is a good tactic, and you will see reference to this in other parts of this book. With no electronic communication available, the group will have to do everything by planning or use couriers, which is anything but ideal but is how things have been done in critical situations for thousands of years.

  - A good technique here is that by SOPs (Standard Operating Procedures), when returning to the survival location, all gathering party routes go through a planned area out of sight of the survival location and rally point. This area is where the part of the group that had to evacuate the site would leave a prearranged signal for the gathering party to go to the rally point. This is easily done in urban areas and can work in rural areas. This is basic group protection. No one should have to live under these conditions, but if a long-term survival situation presents itself, plans and actions such as this will be forced on groups if they want to Survive While Surviving.

- If the gathering party is ambushed, several possible results could happen, and all would put the group into disarray. Without communication, the part of the group securing the survival location would not know what was happening—except that the gathering party did not return. Everyone in the party could have been killed. All or part of the party may have escaped and are going to the rally point. This should be planned if anyone is ambushed. This prevents the ambushers from following the survivors back to the survival location.

- The gathering party could be forced to move in a direction away from the survival location and the location of some members might be unknown. The group securing the survival location would have some serious decisions to make. One would be to send members to check the designated rally point. One might be to go look for the gathering party, and one may be to wait and see what happens. This would depend on available food and water. No positive answers here—the group may have issues in the long run that they won't have the ability to fix.

- If the gathering party gets trapped and cannot return, the survival location group will not know anything unless they have communication. All the possibilities discussed in the previous situations would be in play. The difference here would be that the gathering party may be alive and holding up well but are trapped due to their error or terrain—it makes no difference. You can plainly see without communication, dire decisions will have to be made. Only history will record how they come out.

- If the gathering party has run into trouble and comes straight back to the survival location with casualties, they are probably being hard-pressed if they could not get to the rally point. At this point, the survival location party assists the gathering party and does what they have to do to stop the looters. Casualties will also have to be attended to. If the gathering party returned without food and water, the fate of the group may or may not hang in the balance. The decision on what the group has to do next will hinge on the looters' ability to lay siege to the survival site and how much food and water is on hand to feed the group. There are no good answers here. Maybe the group wins, but maybe they don't.

- If one of the gathering party returns with news that looters have trapped the gathering party at a known location, this will probably be the easiest decision. The group, for what it is worth, has valid communication and knows at least what the situation was when the group member left the gathering party. To help the gathering party, a quick plan is needed, but we need to know a few things.

  - How far away is the gathering party? If they are a few blocks away, the survival location group needs to start the fight with the necessary weapons.

  - If they are two days' travel out, they need to take all their protective gear and extra ammunition. They also need to know what shape the group was in when last seen, how many casualties there were, and their ammunition and water status.

Did they have a plan to break out if they could, and what route were they going to use to get to the rally point? If the group broke out, the planned route to the rally point should be the route the rescue group follows. These are hard tactical decisions that must be made quickly by group leaders.

- What group members will be left to guard the survival location, or is it worth taking everyone and either hoping for the best or moving to a new location? This depends on how much critical equipment is in the survival location that cannot be transported. If the group going to rescue the gathering party will be gone several days, that would certainly put the group left at the survival location in a serious situation unless the group was a big one. Whether traveling or in the survival location, there should always be a close designated rally point known by all members in case the group is separated by circumstances.

I hope the discussion on these bullet points drives home the importance of protective gear and the need for firearms and ammunition. If vehicles are available, this is a much easier situation for the group to handle. I am told that civilians with no training would not be able to handle a situation like we are discussing. I agree to a point, but dire situations sometimes bring natural leadership to the front and untested individuals can save the day.

If disaster struck today, I think only groups that were trained and had some experienced people would make good decisions here. Any untrained group would probably be paralyzed by indecision, but the exception would be my comment on natural leadership as a possibility. There is still time to prepare and get some training, but the ones who do train and start preparing may still fail and be lost to history. Trained and prepared groups are at the mercy of fate and luck and may still perish. If you are a student of history, you know that in the past entire civilizations have perished or disappeared. This would certainly be possible in a worldwide disaster and could happen in a national disaster under the right circumstances.

This book is designed to open up thought processes and enhance training time; all situations presented here could easily be trained on intensely in a paintball or range environment. I suggest choreographed walk-through training first, then paintball, and then range. I also hope that some semblance of order continues to exist after disaster and groups caught up in violent situations could depend on help coming from other responsible people in whatever is left of society. However, experience based on history tells me that if the lights go out nationally and stay out for a year or more, things are going to get rough all the way around.

I would like to leave the uninitiated who are reading this book some thoughts on individual protective equipment. No matter what you have, it is your lifeline to Surviving While Surviving. Following are some points that have been driven home many times over in my career by trainers and soldiers with vastly more experience than I.

- Keep your weapons on you or at arm's reach.
- Clean and maintain your weapons religiously, including magazines.
- Do not use corroded or dirty ammunition.
- When taking equipment out of your rucksack or backpack, put it back in as soon as you are finished.
- All guns are always loaded—treat them as such.
- If you take off any gear, have it so you can get it quickly. Never have it scattered or in disarray.
- Whatever gear you put on your combat harness or utility belt should not interfere with other gear that may have to be used quickly.
- If you are carrying gear you are not using, why are you carrying it?
- All equipment gets heavy when you're tired, but equipment should be comfortable when you are not tired.
- If in a bad area, sleep with your boots on. Never sleep without someone on guard.
- If you have well-trained small units, you automatically have well-trained large units.
- The people that sweat and bleed in training will bleed less in combat.

Never sleep without someone on guard. (mediaphotos, courtesy of iStock)

If you pay attention to these bullet points, you will be heading in the right direction. I had always heard that if things are going to go wrong in a tactical situation, they will go wrong at the worst possible time. I have found this to be true on numerous occasions. No one can predict what our future holds, but we are at a time in our history where things are taking place that could not have been imagined fifty years ago.

We now have sheriffs and police chiefs on national television telling the citizens in their cities and counties to arm themselves and be ready to protect themselves. This is being said in a time before disaster, so I do not even want to think what will happen to the unprepared after disaster. It is human nature that necessary things we do not like or look on as difficult are sometimes put off or studiously ignored. What we are talking about in this book—the need to prepare—is one of those tasks. Depending on where you live, you are facing sure disaster in the future. I am not a weatherman or prophet, but I would suggest that another storm along the lines of Katrina or Sandy is in the future. I would also say that having prepared for disaster does not mean your stores will not end up downwind or underwater if you do not evacuate when ordered. Having your survival gear packed in vehicles makes evacuation easy and safer for all. I also know that this may not be possible for one-vehicle families or families depending on public transportation, but again I have no good answers.

Chapter Seven

Group Survival Equipment

In the last chapter, I covered my take on individual protective equipment. I have mixed feelings on what I am going to say next because of the different ways people look at things. There will be a group that will say the most important thing in a survival situation is food and water, and they would be right—all the survival books say so. The survival books also say fire and shelter are very important, and they are right.

My take on the national disaster we are talking about in this book is that guns and ammunition are the most important. I say this because when a breakdown of society happens, if you do not have guns and ammunition, it makes no difference how much food and water you have. Eventually someone else will be eating and drinking it if you do not have the means to stop them from taking it.

You can starve to death while having all the guns and ammunition you need. But in the situation we are talking about, I will go with guns and ammunition because with them I can always get food and water. Let's leave that right there.

I have presented information to evoke some serious thinking on group and individual protective gear and individual equipment to Survive While Surviving. It's time to think of the long haul—we are going to prepare for a year of survival in our planned survival location. If you are planning a move to a remote location, take a look at group vehicles and what they are going to carry. Some changes may be made in the preparatory phase, which is hopefully taking place now. What is the group going to need to make it a year? In urban areas, where are you going to cache survival gear? If it all goes to pieces, can you stock enough to keep you and the group going? We're going to start out with the really serious stuff: food and water.

Food

I am told that to stay healthy you should be taking in at least one thousand to twelve hundred calories a day. This means in the preparatory phase, we really need to consider what we store for food. Being from a military background, I would immediately think of MREs (Meals Ready to Eat). They are heavy on calories and sustain combat troops in the field. They also have a five-year shelf life, so if you're decent at math and know you are stocking up for a year, you should be okay. I have seen people buy MREs and when they got to their home, the meals were already past their shelf-life date. I have eaten MREs past their shelf life, and in my experience they haven't killed me. However, I am an old soldier—I like C rations. There are better foods that will last longer and are better for you, including the following food types.

Freeze-Dried Foods

Just add boiling water and let simmer. Some out there have a twenty-five-year shelf life, and they taste good. They come in easily stackable military-grade packaging and will give you some of the calories you need. I'm told some are better than others. I suggest trying a few out and make your own decisions. How many will you need? I say two per day per group member, so do the mathematics. If you are going to move them, make sure you have the cargo space or storage space in your survival location. I am still researching these, but they look promising from a survival standpoint.

Some people will say the most important thing in a survival situation is food and water, and they would be right. The survival books also say fire and shelter are very important, and they are also right. (Dale C. Spartas/http:// www.spartasphoto.com)

Dried Beans

There are several different dried beans that will fit your survival needs. Historically, beans have been keeping people alive for thousands of years. They are certainly much cheaper than freeze-dried foods. They must be kept dry when stored but will last as long as you need them. Pinto, red, and lima beans are my personal favorites. There are people who do not like beans or may have allergies to them, and I understand that. If you don't have allergies to a particular bean but just don't like them, I will tell you that if disaster strikes and goes long term, you will gladly eat them. Rice and beans are both nutritious yet inexpensive foods that, when combined, form a complete protein and contain some sodium. Additional information can be readily found online. I say store everything in metal containers, as once disaster strikes mice and rats will become a major problem. Metal containers will keep them from getting into your food stores.

Rice

White rice has also been a staple for thousands of years; it's cheap and can be stored for an indefinite time. I am still researching this. I am told that it should be stored with oxygen absorbers, but I wonder how people in the old days managed to get by without them. Rice, like beans, must be kept dry or it will spoil. There are now a myriad of watertight containers for food storage available, and again I recommend metal containers. Brown rice has oils in it that will turn rancid over time. People have told me they do not like rice, but I guarantee if they haven't eaten in five days and someone gives them rice, they will like it. Another plus for standard white rice is it contains almost the recommended daily dose of salt (sodium).

Buckwheat

This grain-like food is used heavily in Russia and some Asian countries. It is more nutritious than grain and can be used in a multitude of ways. America produces around seventy-plus tons a year. It stores for the long term and has a short growing season. Most Americans know little to nothing about buckwheat, but I think it's worth the time to research and give it a try.

These are not the only foods you will want or need, but they are, with the exception of freeze-dried foods, centuries-old staples that have saved populations from certain extinction. In an urban environment—because of rats, which are in abundance—all foods should be stored in metal containers on pallets to ensure that it does not spoil and to keep vermin from gnawing through to eat it. Now let's talk a little about the trouble you could have on a move to your remote location. The food needs to be stored in an airtight container in a dry environment. If you are ambushed or your vehicles get shot up en route to your survival site, a detailed check of all storage containers needs to be made to ensure there are no breaks or bullet holes in them that will let your food go bad or be invaded by vermin. You are never going to have enough food stored in a survival situation, so you do not want part of what you have to spoil because you did not check.

Water

This is an absolute no-brainer whether you are in an urban or rural setting. Water means you may live if other things go right, but without it you are going to die. I have mentioned before the ways to ensure you have water. If buying land in a rural area, make sure there is a water source on it. Also, in your move or stored at your site, you need to have plastic sheets or tarps and as many barrels as you can get with sealed tops for collecting rainwater. If you are in an urban area, if you have a flat roof this should be a garden and rainwater gathering area. If you have a yard, the same thing should be taking place. After some time in a survival situation, things are going to get bad, and you are going to have to guard your water or someone else will be drinking it.

If you are moving to a rural site and it has water on it, you can reduce the weight you have to transport and gain space on vehicles by not transporting tons of water. If your water collection barrels have removable tops, you can store equipment in them for the move to make more room. If you are ambushed or shot up on the move, check all containers to ensure they are functional. If transporting water, the check should be easy—if water is leaking out of the truck bed, your containers have been hit. When making the move, all canteens or hydro-packs should be full, and a full five-gallon can or two should be on each vehicle.

If you just eat rice and beans and have water to drink, you will live a long time. Some doctor or scientist may prove me wrong, but if it comes to it, I will chance it. Living where I do, supplementing them with meat will not be a problem. Let's talk about something most people do not think of when it comes to preparing for survival. In short-term survival it makes no difference, but in the long term, it's the difference between maintaining some health and maybe staying alive.

Salt

Few people think of salt when thinking of survival, and in a short-term situation it doesn't make a difference. In the long term, salt, or sodium, becomes a two-edged sword. If you are not getting enough, you could die. However, if you're getting too much, you could get sick and maybe die. If you are salt deficient, you have a condition known as hyponatremia, and you are in trouble. When your salt levels are good, all vital body functions are working, such as proper blood volume and your electrolytes functioning properly. If salt levels are low, seizures and coma are possible. I suggest having a good supply of salt on hand, and use it like you do now. Mineral streams may be a source, as they also contain various levels of sodium. I am told the daily dose of salt should be a level teaspoon, which is approximately 1200 mg.

Iodine

Iodine is an element that is needed for the production of thyroid hormones. The body does not make iodine, but it is an essential part of your diet. Iodine is found in various foods that may be difficult to come by in a survival situation. If you do not have enough iodine in your body, you cannot make enough thyroid hormones. Iodine deficiency can lead to enlargement of the thyroid, hypothyroidism, and to mental retardation in infants and children whose mothers were iodine deficient during pregnancy. Make sure iodized salt is on the list of items added to your food storage.

I put these foods as group survival equipment to drive home the fact that it is an individual and group daily responsibility to acquire and maintain the food supply—both by gathering after disaster and preparing nonperishable food stores prior to disaster.

I don't want to be redundant or spend a lot of time telling people how they should prepare, but the lists in this book are for readers to think about what they may need. This is why we will go over a couple more items on those lists. First, I want to fill in some of the gaps in what you may need for containers to trap rainwater. Trapping water in five-gallon cans makes it easy to carry, but water barrels will hold more. Even with a water source on your property, that doesn't mean nature will not take it away. If in the city, water will be at a premium once it's shut off.

If you only have five-gallon cans, once they are full, you are done collecting water. Any rain that happens after that is wasted on the ground. If you also have water barrels, you can continue to collect water for drinking, gardening, and barter material, especially in cities. If you are planning on moving full water barrels, a good dolly should be in your plans. I suspect water will be worth more than gold in cities. Once you start to barter water, you need to put on your tactical hat, as it will not be lost on anyone that if you have water to barter, you have a lot more where that came from. Everyone who knows you are bartering water will be looking for your survival location and the water in it. You are most likely going to have to defend it quickly.

In the early days of a long-term survival situation when people still have hope, gold and silver will be great barter material. As time goes by and real hunger and thirst are the primary concerns, people will rightfully determine that neither gold nor silver can be boiled, baked, fried, or eaten. What people will want to barter is water, food, medicine, fuel, good shoes, clothing, and anything that shoots. Firewood may also be big. I suspect gold and silver will get you either laughed at or run out of town. If you have it, I would suggest using it early on. Think about it this way: you have not eaten in several days and someone wants to give you gold or silver for a pair of boots. The question is, from a survival standpoint, are you still starving or can you eat the gold?

I've put lists in previous chapters to make you think. There will never be enough equipment, materials, or group capability to cover all the life-threatening situations that may arise in a long-term survival situation. The lists provided are to give you and the group a measuring stick to determine what you can do for yourself and the group in the unending work of acquiring what you will need to Survive While Surviving. Once you begin to stock up on food, water, tools, and all the other things you need to support a lifestyle while surviving, you will quickly realize, especially in urban areas, that it will most likely take more room than you currently have. There are going to be several ways of looking at this problem, but none of them are really the best answer. Depending on the local situation in your area, there may be no answer at all.

Let's start with the one- or two-room apartment in a building with several other apartments in it. No one- or two-room apartments are going to store all that is needed. You will look like a hoarder and will not be able to move around, defend the location, or find specific needed items. It should not be lost on anyone that it will take all occupants of the building working together to have any chance of success and survival. Good tactical planning must be a part of everything you do in preparation for disaster. A good plan would be for all rooms in the building that do not have windows or outside access to be used as storage rooms. The cellar and attic, if they exist, may also be feasible for storage. The rest of the building's rooms would be used for living, light storage, work areas, and defense. There needs to be a plan for storage so things that will be needed regularly are easily accessible. Even though the room may become very full of what is needed, there needs to be walkways for movement so needed materials can be easily found. Food, water, and other critical equipment should not all be stored in one apartment or location in the building. **Note:** All food and water should be stored in metal containers, as rats will be a problem. We have discussed this before—it is critical to survival when long-term storage is required. Rat poison and a pellet gun should be on hand to deal with this problem.

All storage should be on the upper floors with the first floor being used for living, light storage, and defense of the structure. The cellar may also be used, but any street access into the area must be blocked. Should disaster happen, a lot of construction is going to have to take place for there to be any chance of successfully defending the survival location. The research I have done leads me to believe that the part of the population who live in these structures are the most at risk if disaster strikes. The reason is a large percentage of residents are day shoppers with little food on hand, and as a group they are unarmed or have just a few weapons and little ammunition. Many live alone with little to no support from large families or groups. Added to these problems, the work needed to stock up supplies and prepare the structure for defense is almost impossible for the occupants of these structures. It can be done, but only by people with the right mind-set who are willing to pull together as a group.

All is not lost if people pull together and get the process moving. I also hope that the existing infrastructure of government and local services holds together, but only history will record this. I have no idea how much experience in tactics and planning is available, but expect, as in all population groups in the country, some exists. Finances will surely be another problem that there are no good answers for. Only time will record how this part of the population fares if disaster strikes.

I hope the chapter on urban survival locations and the lists provided give the people who read this book as good a start as possible. After disaster strikes, all that has been discussed here may come to pass.

There is no way a single book is going to cover every situation. If your first thought is that what you want to accomplish is not possible, you have a good chance of being right. Groups can usually overcome many obstacles that an individual cannot. I also know that when a group decides to do it and is under pressure of injury or death, amazing things can be done in short order. Having the proper survival mind-set will go a long way toward ensuring both individual and group survival.

Going along with group equipment, let's look at another item on our planning lists. Will I have to repair and maintain weapons? Yes.

Necessary Equipment

- Repair and parts manuals for every gun the group has
- Armorer's tool kit
- Spare parts: firing pins, extractors, ejectors, springs, retaining pins, sights, etc.
- Cleaning rods, bore brushes, rags, and patches for every caliber the group has
- Gun oil, powder solvent, lead solvent, gun grease
- Personal cleaning kit for each gun
- Workbench and storage area for the equipment

If you have the above in a long-term survival situation, you will be light-years ahead of almost everyone else. Within the community that I trust and have had the privilege to be part of, there are many outlooks on weapons and what is best for a group. One view is that all assault rifles should be the same—either M4, AK, etc. This means all weapons the group has have the same spare parts, magazines, and ammunition. I support this view. If you think about it, this should be carried out throughout the group's on-hand weaponry. All combat pistols should be from the same manufacturer and take the same ammunition. All hunting rifles, .22 weapons, shotguns, bows, and pellet guns should be from the same manufacturer. This cuts down on the amount of spare parts and cleaning gear and makes it easy to resupply group members who are running out of ammunition in a fight.

When starting survival and tactical preparation, I know that funds will be at a premium. This will affect every group and individual that is preparing and not wealthy. Hopefully we have time to do what must be done, but we have no way to tell how much time we have. But you may be in better shape than you realize. If you own a gun and it is one not mentioned in this book, you still have what you need to defend yourself. Start buying ammunition for it and make sure you have cleaning materials and a means to carry it—either a sling or holster. What you currently own, you do not have to spend money on to acquire. Learn to use it to its best advantage.

Do not bring a pistol to a long-range rifle fight. I have been in discussions where the weapon of choice for survival is a .22 rifle and a pistol. This is because you can carry a ton of ammunition, as both weapons take the same round and can be used for hunting and defense. I have no argument with this concept in a survival situation, but I believe from a tactical standpoint this option takes a lot of combat capability away from the group. I repeat, in a long-term survival situation, you will be in combat, and you will be engaged by trained people at long range.

Let's look at another question. What can I hunt with to save ammunition?

- Bow and arrows
- Pellet guns
- Spears
- Tomahawks or hatchets
- Traps and snares
- Slingshots
- Rocks

I think you get the idea. These things take practice, patience, time, and developed skill. There are other exotic weapons, such as boomerangs and blowguns, that have been used successfully by tribes around the world. If you have skills with these, that would be another step toward success and a needed talent to survive. Do not go out and buy a spear, as one can easily be made with any fixed-blade knife. There are schools and data on how to build traps and snares and how to use them in any situation—survival or sport. For rocks, tomahawks, and spears, only a good arm, hand-eye coordination, and stealth are required to be successful. If planning on using a bow and arrows, extra strings, arrows, and any spare parts should be on hand.

I am sure at this time, with the list of items we have covered, you have an understanding that one of the things that must be organized, monitored, and adjusted as needed is the storage of your materials. If moving to a rural area, what can go on the vehicles and where? If in a one- or two-room apartment building, what rooms get what and why? Organization here will save time and frustration when things start happening. If a solar flare knocks out all electricity and vehicles, what is the plan if you were planning to move? There will be times where you will need to find something in what you have stored quickly, but if it is not organized this will never happen. In the wrong circumstances, this could be a group disaster requiring emergency actions not planned for. This almost ensures they will not go well.

As in all things of a critical nature, incidents will happen that the group has not planned for or are first-time situational circumstances that the group has no experience in. If this should happen, the stronger the group is, the better chance they have to react to it. There are no guarantees here. I suspect in the past, groups exposed to this misfortune decided it was better to move out of the area, and this may have been the right decision. The problem here is in not knowing what to expect. The group is stuck with having to react to the situation and make a decision as the incident happens. We do things better when we have had time to think about them—and maybe rehearse them—but I can assure you in a disaster situation that will not always be the norm.

Chapter Eight

Movement and Tactics

I do not like discussing tactics, as most professionals consider themselves experts. In my view, I am not an expert. If you have not been in every situation possible, you are not an expert, and very few people have. If you have been, you are only an expert at what you did there. If you are alive, it worked, but I personally shy away from the term. What we are talking about in this book has never happened in our history, and if it does, I would be willing to call groups and individuals who are alive at the end of it experts. With that in mind, I still do not like discussing tactics but look on it as a necessary evil.

With that being said, let's look at some basics that have worked well in the past. For you pros and those that are prepared, this is not for you. All movement is conducted while using tactics to support it, hence the phrase tactical movement. I am a career soldier, so I will draw heavily from that experience and what has worked for me in combat situations. Let's first start with group movement, such as what will have to take place with gathering parties. For the currently untrained, our movement formation will depend on several things.

Factors Influencing Movement

- Enemy capability—looters and raiders
- Terrain you have to move through—urban, rural, open, forested, or restricted
- Number in moving group and their capabilities

With these factors in mind, I will describe some formations that are used by the military.

- Wedge formation
- File formation
- Line formation

We are going to stick with these three. They are basic formations used when moving, attacking, and moving through restricted terrain. I will explain the basics to you, and it will be up to you to practice and perfect your group's knowledge. Keep in mind that when moving outside your survival location, you are in enemy territory. You could be attacked at any time from long or extremely close range. One thing to keep in mind is what the formation and each individual's position and dispersion in it are for. This is for all-around observation and security of the formation and ensuring the whole formation cannot be fired on at one time. That's the plan, but I can tell you if caught in a well-prepared ambush, the whole formation may find itself under fire. When moving tactically, no one moves unless covered by someone else. Review pictures of army wedge formation online, and everything from team, squad, and platoon will come up. A team is four or five men, a squad is ten men, and a platoon could be as many as forty or fifty.

All these formations look good on paper, but in reality every man in the formation should be able to see the man in front of him. The formation should not get so spread out that the line of sight is lost. Once that happens, the unit's all-around security, observation, and ability to fire is lost. Let's cover formation use and why we have different ones for different situations. Do not forget in your gathering party formations that members may be pushing carts or carrying heavy loads that prevent them from being ready to defend the formation.

Wedge Formation

This formation gives the group the ability to observe and fire 360 degrees. The entire formation can fire to the front and rear, and half the formation can fire left and right while staying in the formation. We have used this wedge in open terrain, in woods with good visibility between trees, on city streets, in hill country, and in limited visibility. As in all formations, when visibility diminishes or terrain closes in, the distance between formation members is tightened up. The distance between formation members could be five meters or fewer or out to fifteen or more meters. For survival purposes, any number of members could be in this formation. If there are a large number in the formation, I suggest two or more wedges with as much distance as terrain allows between the wedges. If one wedge runs into looters and has to fire with multiple wedges, one can be firing while the others move. This needs to be practiced before the event. Paintball exercises are excellent for this training.

File Formation

This formation is used in restricted terrain and during reduced visibility. The formation members can observe and fire left or right of the formation but have little capability to the front and rear. We use this formation in thick woods or bushes, in fog, snow, night, and extremely narrow city streets and alleys. The distance between formation members is usually line of sight. This is not considered a good combat formation, although maneuvering out of this formation has been done when fired on by the enemy. In your search engine, type in "army file formation" to see pictures. This formation is where breaks in contact are frequent during reduced visibility. Moving at night through woods almost ensures breaks in the formation if tight control is not used. Even then, breaks in contact between members are common.

Line Formation

This formation is used as an assault or search tactic. The formation can place heavy firepower to the front or rear but has little to no combat power left and right. The formation will support fire and movement or fire and maneuver. In your search engine, type in "army line formation" or "fire and maneuver." This formation is usually controlled by leaders in the rear of the formation ensuring one part of the formation does not get too far out front or fall behind. As in all formations, the more practice you get, the better you conduct this move. Individual members should not get tunnel vision or target fixation but should stay somewhat aware of where they are in the move. Paintball exercises and movement over varied terrain should be practiced by the group.

Fire and Movement

Individual formation members make short rushes forward while supported by other members or a section of the line makes a short rush while supported by the non-rushing section. Varied terrain, short rolling hills, or raises in the ground sometimes make this a difficult tactic, as the supporting part of the movement will temporarily lose sight of the moving part, which can result in friendly fire casualties when using live fire, which no one wants or can afford regardless of the situation.

Fire and Maneuver

A section of the line will maneuver left or right to advance on the enemy flank while being supported by the rest of the line. This is a standard infantry tactic that has been used in fields, on hills, in cities, and anywhere the terrain will support the formation's use. The same disastrous friendly fire accidents can take place here if the maneuver element location is lost to sight and they reappear in the impact zone of the supporting group members. This has happened occasionally with well-trained military units.

There is also squad or unit overwatch and bounding overwatch tactics. Part of the unit will move to a designated point on the ground while covered by the overwatching part of the unit. The bounding overwatch uses either successive or alternate bounds. This depends on terrain and weapons capability. Review this online by searching images of bounding overwatch. Practice these moves with paintballs. Keep in mind that leaders have to control this formation in a survival situation just as they do in a military action. If radios are not available, this would be extremely difficult and require constant training or rehearsals. Maneuvering out of these formations can be either toward or away from the enemy. I have already cautioned about getting into sustained fights, as ammunition will be an issue, as well as casualties and their evacuation under extreme conditions. I suggest ensuring that you have members in the group that were in combat arms while in the service, as it would be in the group's best interest. If the moving formation is a gathering party with carts or other means of hauling equipment and the formation is fired on, the formation engages the enemy while the carts get to safety. If the situation calls for the group to move forward toward the enemy, the members with carts give what support they can from their position and then follow the attack at as safe a distance as would be prudent based on the situation and terrain.

Note: No survival group is ever going to be able to use the ammunition expenditures the military does. Prolonged engagements will quickly cause any group, no matter how well prepared, to run out of ammunition.

It is extremely hard to talk in detail, as the formation could get into trouble in a wide variety of terrain and obstructed-area situations. There are no perfect answers other than pick good leaders, train, prepare every chance you get, and talk out and rehearse every move. There are other tactical options that will and can be used in a long-term survival situation; these are recon and security patrols, ambushes, and raids. My intent here is not to make everyone reading this book into a commando, but basic knowledge on these tactics may be the difference between living and dying. They will be an important part of your group's capabilities that will go a long way toward ensuring that you Survive While Surviving. Remember that there will be looter and raider groups that also know these tactics and will employ them against you.

Recon Patrols

In the world of infantry, combat recon patrols are used to find out where the enemy is, what they are doing, and what their capabilities and intentions are. In a long-term survival situation where violence is taking place, nothing about recon patrols should change. You are just using them against a different enemy, which would be looters and raiders. You would also use them to determine if an area or group of people were safe or a threat. A group conducting recon or security patrols is certainly less likely to be surprised by looters or raiders. The bigger the group, the more successful they will be.

Requirements to Conduct a Good Recon Patrol

- Know where you are going, how you are getting there, and what equipment you will need. (Have you heard this before?)

- Be able to make a good tactical movement.

- Be able to move with stealth as a group and an individual.

- Be proficient in camouflage.

- Be able to observe without being detected.

- If detected, be able to make a good, covered withdrawal without getting decisively engaged—which is easier said than done in certain situations.

A good way to train is with ex-military veterans in a paintball scenario. Find out what it takes to be stealthy in moving on a group and observing them without being detected. These requirements will change drastically as terrain changes. Also get to know what your personal and physical limits are. Remember you are not invisible; you must develop the skills to be successful when operating against

In the world of infantry, combat recon patrols are used to find out where the enemy is and what they are doing. (zabelin, courtesy of iStock)

people who may know as much as you do, if not more. The move from paintballs to bullets is easy. The difference is engagements with bullets produce permanent results.

Security Patrols

You would use security patrols around your survival location. These are small patrols of a few group members that would go beyond the survival location to determine if the location was being approached by looters or raiders. They might set up in a location where they can monitor movement over a wide area. They should be armed and ready to run into looters or raiders. Remember, if outside the survival location, carry seventy-two hours of survival and protective gear.

Requirements for Conducting a Good Security Patrol

- Know where you are going, how you are getting there, and what equipment you need. (I think you have heard this before.)

- Be able to conduct a good tactical small group move in which no one moves unless covered by someone else.

- Be able to move with stealth as an individual and small group.

- Be able to hide and observe without being detected.

- Be able to escape if detected without getting decisively engaged.

Security patrols are small with just a few members. The training recon patrol members take is the same for security patrols. Both patrols are noncombat oriented, and their intent should be not to make any contact or be detected. This is easier done in a rural area than an urban area. Keep in mind, this is a short-range area patrol. Also remember the intent of your plan may be overrode by looter or raider actions.

Ambushes

Military manuals say an ambush is a surprise attack against a moving or temporarily halted enemy. In our case, that would be looters or raiders. Ambushes can be conducted on roads, trails, city streets, or any place the group knows looters or raiders would be moving. The ambush should not be detected until the group is ready to fire; camouflage is imperative here. Ambush location versus terrain is important. Once initiated, the ambush must be conducted with extreme violence and all the firepower the group can deliver. Do not waste ammunition here. You will know fairly quickly if the ambush was successful. A lack of return fire generally means success. The kill zone should be under observation by all group members. If this is not possible due to terrain, the ambush leader should position him- or herself where he or she can see most if not all of the kill zone. Again, terrain may prevent this.

Requirements for a Successful Ambush

- It must remain undetected until initiated.
- It must be initiated with maximum accurate firepower.
- It must be a complete surprise.
- The terrain and its surroundings must support the ambush position.
- Security should be in place to secure the ambush site.

The ambush should have left, right, and rear security. All members of the ambush should know the withdrawal route and the designated rally point. In a survival situation, all weapons, ammunition, and equipment of those ambushed should be taken by the ambush members. I do not think, as in some military ambushes, that you will have to worry about a reaction force of looters or raiders, but leave security in place while taking the weapons and equipment from the kill zone. Do not assume anything. Again, the best way to train is with ex-military combat arms members and paintball exercises. If you cannot do it with paintballs, you cannot do it with bullets.

Ambushes have historically been either single-point or area ambushes, where several ambushes are put out on different trails or roads in the same area. Hopefully, radio communication will be available. If not, group leaders must have control of the group and develop signals to alert the group for needed actions. The ambush should be initiated by gunfire that keys all members to fire into the kill zone. I am still hopeful that some semblance of order will prevail after disaster strikes, but based on past world and national history, I am not confident this will take place.

Raids

Raids are probably the oldest tactic in history. People, tribes, and countries have been raiding each other since we came out of caves—and

I suspect while we were still in caves. Raids have been used to attack and destroy a certain site, to attack and occupy a site, or to attack a site and take materials that are in it. In a long-term survival situation, looters and raiders will conduct a raid where and when they find a survival location. Survival groups that are running out of available food and water will conduct a raid if one of their members or a recon patrol finds an area where there is food and water owned by someone else. That's the way desperate people act in life-threatening situations.

Requirements for a Successful Raid

- There must be knowledge of the raid location.
- A good tactical plan must be developed.
- The raid force must get to the location undetected.
- They must have surprise and firepower.

Training for raids can be done with paintballs and should be accomplished on various terrain and buildings. Groups preparing for disaster can take training days and use half the day for raids or ambushes and the other half for patrol training. Training should be done in daylight first and then at night. In cities and large population areas, these tactics would be used the most in a survival situation, but groups in rural areas should also be proficient in these tactics. Living life like we do now is easy, but having to survive day to day while tactically securing yourself would be hard even on professionals. I believe among the majority of the population, only the ones who have a true survival mentality and the ability to adapt will be successful. Again, there is no really good news here. How will these tactics help the survivalist?

They will teach that armed mobs with little dispersion or control of their firepower are easily defeated by organized groups. This has taken place throughout history and continues today in Syria, Iraq, and other areas of the world. Training is the difference. Another reason survival groups need to learn these tactics and how to fight as a unit is that they will be facing trained and armed groups as time passes and things continue to fall apart. These armed groups may be ex–military members, preppers that have trained for this event, and, as I have already mentioned, drug cartels and street gangs. In the long run, if the situation lasts months, we are all going to become raiders or looters.

In the cities, these gangs will become a force to be reckoned with by all citizens whether they are prepared or not. As disaster lengthens and food and water become harder to get, these gangs will become raiders using their own recon patrols to find groups and areas of activity. Sooner or later, everyone is going to have to deal with this situation whether they want to or not. The groups that are trained the best, armed, and with the right survival mind-set will do the best against them.

As in all events such as those we are discussing, the group being attacked is most likely going to sustain casualties—both wounded and dead. I am still hopeful that within the cities there will be places the wounded could be treated, but over time supplies will be depleted. If these places do exist, they will be forced to practice medicine as they did hundreds of years ago. The most likely scenario is that the group will take care of its wounded and hurt to the best of its ability and will have to watch the critically injured die. I would like to tell everyone that in preparation you could learn surgery, but I cannot. You might be able to learn to suture a wound, take out a tooth, or perform other minor surgeries, but learning major surgery requires going to medical school. If you are in medical school, you will not have time to do any other preparation, although a group that has a doctor in it should go to great lengths to ensure that the individual is protected and kept out of firefights as much as possible. In a fight, good tactics would suggest the trained group member does not run out into gunfire to help casualties but instead casualties are brought to him or her in a secure location. You only have to look at the high percentage of combat medics and corpsmen who become casualties to know that this is good advice.

We have talked about tactics for the gathering party, as they are the ones that will be moving through the terrain and have the best chance of ending up in a shooting situation. However, the survival location is another place where the group needs to look at some tactics to support their defense of the location. In the event that some members have to leave the location, there should be a plan to support that move. If the move is to go out and get weapons and equipment dropped by attackers, group members in the survival location should be in firing positions and observing for danger before any move outside is made. Group members who are to cover the move should be in two or more positions. If there is an upper floor, there should be cover positions there. While this is happening, the other sides of the location should have group members covering them. You can see from this requirement why a small group would be ineffective.

In a survival situation, the best weapons for covering members would be hunting rifles with scopes. This is because any fire from any member should have an excellent chance of hitting the target with the first shot. The military uses M4s, squad automatic weapons, and machine guns to supply suppressive fire to support a move. In a survival situation, your suppressive fire needs to be your first round hitting and killing what you are shooting at. You will not have the luxury of automatic suppressive fire, but if you do, you should still not be wasting ammunition you will need later. In the military, if I was running out of ammunition in a fight, a radio call would generally get a helicopter and ammunition supply fairly quickly. In a survival situation, that is not going to happen. If you think times were hard when you had ammunition, you are not going to believe what needs to happen when you run out. You may want to review movies such as *The Last Samurai*, as things are going to get very up close and personal, and you may find yourself violating the cardinal rule of not bringing a knife to a gunfight.

When leaving the survival location, you are in danger of being ambushed as soon as the group is outside the location. This, of course, depends on the surrounding area supporting an ambush position. In time the survival location will become well known to anyone in the area, therefore the chance of being attacked or ambushed while leaving or returning is good. A tactical move out of the location is in the group's best interests. Before departing, binoculars and scopes should be used to determine if an ambush may be present. Any movement should be suspect, and rifles with scopes should keep it under observation. The group leaving the location should leave with good dispersion between members and be covered by the rest of the group in the location. I feel this lifestyle of constant threats will affect all group members, and they will develop a siege mentality where they do not venture from the survival location. This will, of course, result in running out of food and water. Once this siege mentality starts to set in, leaders must make a decision on moving to a new location. The alternative is to start ambushing or raiding those threatening the group.

I would like to think that these situations would not arise, but if all government control and police services are gone, I cannot see how they will not. In urban areas, one danger may be if a group of looters or raiders sets up in a building that allows them to keep your survival location under observation. This makes them a direct and constant threat to the group that will demand unending occupation and defense of the survival location or a planned raid on the offending location. Group leaders will have to make this decision based on the threat to the group. If the decision is made to try to raid the offending group, several things need to be known. Some can be determined by careful observation while others will have to be determined by recon patrols.

Before Raiding, Consider These Factors

- Is the site fortified?
- Does the group possess the ability to clear the fortifications?
- How are the occupants armed?
- Can the group move on the location without being detected?
- Does the group have the capability to conduct the raid?
- If not, what would be an alternative plan?

Decisions based on these factors may drive the group to decide to move to a new location. This decision may be made because the group determines it cannot get through the location's fortifications, it cannot move on the site without being detected, or it does not want to risk a major fight that may decimate the group. You can see how the decision on group action or survival will be hard and will result in the group moving into an unknown and certainly unforeseen future, but the reality is if we are in a long-term survival situation, we are all in an unforeseen future.

Let's end this chapter with a talk about a move made from the chosen survival location. Whether a move for the benefit of the group is from food and water running out at the present location or for tactical reasons makes no difference, we are still going to have to move. First, never go anywhere without a plan, so where have we planned to go? Whether it is near or far, we have to look at what we have to get to the new location and how we will get there. We're in trouble if it's heavy, no vehicles are available, and the new site is a long way away. If it cannot be moved in one load, we have to determine what our options are. Let's say the move is out of the urban area to a rural site, and the move time is six days. This puts it at a twelve-day round trip if we have to return to the original location. This is going to drive some serious group decisions based on the options available and the capability in exercising those options.

Some Reasons to Move

- The move can be done at the group's discretion.
- The move is forced because of food and water being depleted in the area.
- The move is being forced due to an ongoing tactical situation.

Let's take a look at each option, as it will help in the preparation and planning process. There is a danger of paralysis through analysis when planning and preparing. Hopefully, some information will prevent that.

A Move at the Group's Discretion

The only decisions that have to be made here are simple. If we cannot transport everything in one move, how do we handle it?

Group Options

- Does the group make one move with as much survival gear as possible?
- If one move with all survival gear is not possible, is it worthwhile survival-wise and tactically to make additional moves?
- Can any survival gear left be cached until a trip back can be made?
- If not, is it worthwhile to barter it off for needed equipment?
- Should equipment left be destroyed if it cannot be taken?
- Is any of the equipment so critical that a return trip must be made? What group members secure it? Is there enough food and water to sustain them while the others are gone?

As you can see, even with group discretion there are still decisions to be made. If, for instance, an abundance of ammunition was on hand and could not be carried in one trip, this would force additional trips. The question would be with a twelve-day round trip—if nothing went wrong—could the water and food supply sustain the plan? There will always be life or death decisions to be made if a long-term disaster situation is forced on the population.

A Move Because Food and Water Are Depleted

The decisions here are simple—how much food and water is on hand to support the move? If it is not enough for multiple moves, caching what equipment is left may be an option. If it is not, the group should put what is to be done with the equipment that cannot be transported to a group vote. At any rate, if equipment must be left, hard decisions have to be made on what equipment is taken. Keep in mind that if the group gets to the new location, they may not have the capabilities they did before the move. One might consider that if enough critical equipment is being left, it might be better not to move with the understanding that gathering parties would have to be gone longer and probably more often. These will be hard life or death decisions for the group.

A Move Due to an Ongoing Tactical Situation

In this instance, the previously discussed points will be in play, but if the group is being forced to move because of the tactical situation, they may have problems within the group.

Potential Problems

- They are running out of ammunition.
- They do not have the tactical capability to maintain the defense of their survival location.
- The group has been reduced in number by casualties and can no longer use gathering parties and defend the survival location at the same time.
- They are running out of food and water.

Whatever the reason is, a move is imminent, and decisions will have to be made quickly. These decisions will have to focus on what the group is capable of carrying while maintaining fighting capability and the ability to evacuate the survival location undetected. There are no good answers here. They may escape if the looters or raiders attacking the location are not strong enough to fully surround it, if they can slip away in darkness or inclement weather, or the surrounding terrain and building configuration may assist their withdrawal. Whatever means they use to withdraw, they are just heading for harder times and will eventually either perish, become separated, or link up with another group—only history will tell. If disaster strikes, this situation will take place many times over.

In a true survival situation that goes long term where critical items to support life are suddenly not available, there are certain things that will invariably take place due to the capability of different population groups.

Possible Results of a National Disaster

- Initially, local governments will try to maintain a semblance of order supported by the federal government.

- Initially, as it has in the past, looting and violence will break out in many areas around the country. Local agencies and the federal government will respond to this violence. Due to the national situation, martial law will be declared.

- If the power is out nationally, everyone depending on it for life support will start to die.

- As it always does, violence will beget violence, and looting and riots will spread to cities that initially remained calm.

- If you look at the national map, you will quickly realize violence in our major cities will take all the assets the federal and local governments have.

- Days into the event, security forces may be shooting looters and rioters but will also be taking casualties, thereby being less effective. It is a fact that security forces, both local and government, are vastly outnumbered in all areas of the country.

- At a certain point in the battle to restore order in the cities, some local and federal members are going to realize what is happening nationally and desert to go to their families. They will take their weapons and equipment with them and reduce security force effectiveness even more. These desertions may also be on the civilian official side. If you look at hurricane Katrina, many of the New Orleans police force stayed home to protect their families and homes. This will most likely also happen in a national disaster.

Let's hold with the bullet points and look at what should be the plan for any country, including ours, in a national emergency. When martial law is declared, the first places it will be enforced is in the big cities and metropolitan areas, then the suburban areas, small town America, and finally the rural areas, where we will all hope to be if disaster strikes. There are currently not enough security forces in any country to enforce martial law if the majority of the population is rioting and taking part in looting and violence.

- Days into the event, looters who are tired of getting hammered by still-effective security forces will start moving into suburban areas. This will spread security forces even thinner. Hopefully neighborhood watch groups will have thought about this and be ready to put away their cell phones and get the guns out to start dealing with looters and raiders.

- At an early point, resupply of security forces will become paramount, and convoys will be traversing the road system. These convoys will have to be protected, which will take more security forces out of the fight in the cities and suburbs.

At this point we are at a crossroads—if security forces can restore order, there is hope we can weather this. If they cannot, a total breakdown of society—at least in the metropolitan areas—is likely, and the long dark times will begin. At this point everything we have talked about in this book will come to pass unless luck or fate steps in.

- Initially anyone not armed is in danger of losing their life or being seriously injured. To be truthful, small families and individuals who are armed are also at risk.

- Cities will start to burn, and all supplies will be depleted. Looters and raiders will start attacking each other and move into the suburbs. People who are alone, disabled, or sick will start to die.

- People in small towns and living in rural areas will pull together, and local governments may establish some order. Hopefully a militia will be established to assist the local police and fire departments. Local farmers will pitch in, and some semblance of a food supply, water, and maybe electricity will be available.

- In cities, if gas is in vehicles and they are working, some industrious looters will try to get as far as they can to continue looting. At this time everyone should be on guard and hopefully armed. Survival is going to be a way of life and so will Surviving While Surviving.

After reading these bullet points, you might think certain groups may start this survival situation better off than others as far as armament goes. That thought will be correct and will instantly start to affect everyone in the area.

For instance, what equipment did the deserters take with them? Heavy weaponry and armored vehicles would be one guess. What are the ex-security forces going to do when they get hungry? What are looters and raiders now armed with since they have looted gun stores and possibly supply convoys that were hijacked? From a tactical standpoint—and even if you have prepared and have the weapon mix suggested in this book—you may not be the best armed group in the area. I will say armament is good, but it is only as effective as the user's ability and training to use it.

I am not going to dwell on what caused the national disaster. Whether it was a power grid failure, a financial collapse, or a solar flare that knocks everything out makes no difference if what I have depicted in this book happens. At the end of the good times, if you have not prepared as a nation, state, county or city, or as a group or individual, the game will be on. All of us will be in the same situation, and you will live or die depending on your preparedness, luck, adaptability, and mind-set, but there will be no guarantees. If disaster lasts a year or more, I have no idea what the end result will be. We started in caves, and those of us who are still alive may be back in them.

With that being said, there are certain possibilities if the disaster is only in the United States or North America. These things are certainly worth thinking about regarding what is going to take place with the rest of the world.

Several Possibilities Come to Mind

- A worldwide rescue event is initiated.
- An unfriendly country sees a chance to launch nuclear missiles.
- An unfriendly country decides to invade during this time of crisis.

I will leave it at those three. I can only imagine in the first case response will be slow, incomplete, and uncoordinated, which will cause delays and the initiation of some of the situations we have talked about. In the second case, we as a nation will be finished, and survival options just got fewer. In the third, we have all of the problems discussed in this book plus an ultimate armed gang will be looking to kill us or subjugate us. If a national disaster strikes based on what is currently happening in our world, I guess all of the above three situations could be put down as distinct possibilities.

Chapter Nine

Caches

We have mentioned caches in a couple chapters in this book. I consider caches part of your tactical survival plan. The first question to come up is where do I cache something I will need later? Back when there were fewer people this was fairly easy. Today, with what seems like people being everywhere you go, once you decide on your cache site, the first question should be if anybody is looking and how you should hide it.

Generally, in rural areas it is pretty easy to determine if you are truly alone. In urban areas, with buildings every square inch and thousands of windows someone could be in with binoculars, it is almost impossible to guarantee you are not being observed if you are out on the street. Let's look at some techniques that have worked in the past. We will start with the biggest population areas first.

Caching in an Urban Area

Caching in any urban area is difficult in the respect that it is generally covered in concrete. On the other hand, there are thousands of buildings, vacant lots, yards, and parks that could be used. If your survival location is in an urban area, you may be able to cache close to or at your survival location. From a tactical standpoint, this would possibly be your best option. However, the thought of most looters would be that everything is in the structure, and no thought of an outside cache would even enter their minds. Let's look at buildings in the heart of the city. The first rule of caching is to remember where you put it.

Places to Consider

- **Wooden stairs**—If you pry up a wooden stair, there is generally a good gap under the stairs where anything of moderate size could be stored. The requirement is that nothing should show that the stair was pried up, and it should be secured so it is as stable and tight as the other stairs. There is also a chance the wood may be pried up for fuel if it is a hard winter, and your cache could be discovered.

- **Air conditioning and heating ducts**—These have been used all over the world for hiding contraband and family treasures. The attic or cellar would be the best places to cache anything. In upper rooms would also be good if a duct with a grate was present. If the duct is a vertical duct, the cache material could be hung down into it with a rope or cord. The cord needs to be securely held by a screwed in eyebolt or equivalent, and some trash or other camouflage material needs to be used to conceal the cord.

- **Boilers**—Many older buildings have large boilers for heating the building. Most have access doors into a fairly large space that would be ideal for a cache. With the power out, these boilers would be off. Make sure they are electrically powered and not coal, as survivors could start a warming fire in them if they are. You could even put some rubble in and around the boiler to camouflage the cache. The more it is junked up, the less likely it will be looked at closely.

- **Buildings with courtyards**—Some are concrete, but others are brick, flagstone, or grass. Many have large concrete planters or statues. It should not take too much thought to be able to cache here. This, of course, is an area where you could be under unknown observation. If the building was a group's survival location, being observed by unwanted survivors is not a consideration. The only potential problem here is if raiders run the survival group out of the building and occupy it, getting to the cache may be problematic. Also, the cache may have to be installed during reduced visibility or inclement weather if outside, as it is subject to outsider observation.

- **Parks and vacant lots**—All cities have parks and vacant lots both large and small. These are good places to cache if you are not seen by everyone in town. Late at night may be good. In my experience, if you cache by digging it is extremely difficult to camouflage the dig spot. A good place would be under play stations for children. Clear the safety chips, and if it is not concrete, dig and cache, then put the safety chips back and spread some creative rubble and trash and hope for the best. Do not cache all critical items in one cache site. Vacant lots present many cache potentials, but again you must ask if anyone is watching. The good thing here is that after the disaster, you will not have to worry about a developer building a structure over your cache.

- **Commercial buildings**—There are numerous places in commercial buildings where caches could be positioned. Most commercial buildings are full of machinery, storage materials, small rooms, plumbing pipes, air conditioning vents, etc. There are literally tens of thousands of places where caches could be hidden. Many commercial buildings are full of waste and rubble. If abandoned, these would be excellent places for small and maybe large caches, but do not use rubble that can be burned for heat. The possibilities in these structures are endless—from old chimneys to hidden ledges and oil or wastewater sumps. Careful study of these areas and imagination will give you some great cache sites.

- **Single-dwelling survival locations**—All of these ideas should be considered if they exist in or around the structure. If the location is on a slab or you have a concrete patio, it would be simple to cut out a section of sod, dig under the slab, and cache what you want. Fill the hole and replace the sod. Any sign of caching will soon be erased by nature. You could also put some light rubble over the site to camouflage it. Another good place is under sheds, doghouses, or anywhere on the property that lends itself to your needs that would look normal and not like an obvious cache site. Again, the cache site should be installed at night or in the early hours.

I am sure this opens some thought on caches, but the old standbys of cutting into floors and walls and camouflaging with rubble should not be forgotten. If I were putting in a cache, whether it was outside or inside, I would have the group do several things before and after caching, but you will have to make your own decisions and then roll the dice that they were good ones.

Commercial buildings are often full of waste and rubble. (Lorraine Boogich)

When Caching

- I would do several walk-throughs to assess the site to determine it is what I need.

- Once chosen, I would put the site under twenty-four-hour covert surveillance to see what traffic comes through the area.

- I would wait for a dark or inclement night to install and camouflage the site.

- I would do a walk-through the next day to check the camouflage and have the site under twenty-four-hour covert tactical surveillance.

If the cache was detected going in, it would be dug up immediately by whoever saw the team install it. The surveillance team would be a tactical team that could deal with anyone attempting to dig up or steal the hidden goods to retrieve them for their group's benefit. Some people will say this is paranoid, but I say it is a good, smart tactic in a Survive While Surviving situation. Groups who think this way have a better than average chance of still being alive if the disaster situation ends and normal times return. For example, if your cache of interest has ammunition in it and you are in a fight with looters and are running out of ammunition, the cache is your resupply that will keep you alive. If you get to the cache where you put it and find your ammunition is gone—stolen by someone who observed you putting it in—would these tips have been paranoia or good tactics?

In my world, everything that is cached is in either square or round PVC pipe with end caps and a desiccant bag for absorbing moisture inside. If buried outside, the seal lines on the end caps are sprayed with water seal or bed liner to ensure there is no water leakage into the container. All food is double wrapped and left in its original bags before being placed into the PVC pipe and buried. There are other ways to seal a cache that are easily found on the Internet. I use PVC pipe for its durability, and I can determine the length and shape I need.

Caching in a Rural Area

This should be a safer drill than caching in an urban area, but I would not throw away good tactics here. I would still do my walk-through, observe the site for a day, put it in at night, check the camouflage the next day, and have it under tactical surveillance for a day after the cache was put in. The places available in rural areas are in the millions over several hundred acres.

Where to Cache in Rural Areas

- In and around the survival location
- In burned-out buildings
- In dry streambeds
- Underwater in lakes, ponds, and streams
- Between large boulders in boulder fields
- In hollow trees
- In dense growths of bushes
- Under existing trails or roads
- Under prominent trees on steep slopes
- In swamps or high-water areas

Again, all my caches are in PVC pipe. I usually use square for ammunition in factory boxes, round for weapons and other equipment, and both square and round for food and other needed survival items. Things that are cached underwater are always attached to a hidden pull cord, the PVC has two desiccant bags in it, and the entire PVC package is sprayed with two coats of leak seal. I have not sunk food in water, but I tend to bury it in areas of good drainage and away from areas subject to erosion. There are no guarantees when caching that Mother Nature will not take your cache away. Stay away from avalanche and rock slide areas. Bad flooding during heavy rain years could take your underwater cache away. In dry streambeds, I tend to bury them deep.

Total knowledge of your cache sites is imperative; you should be able to find them in the dark. You should also have them recorded as waypoints on your GPS, though those devices may not be around in a long-term survival situation when batteries run out. I tend to put the cache in at night. If you are putting one in during the day, you should be masked from long-range observation. If you are putting in your cache and one ridgeline over someone is watching with binoculars, unless you are following the recommended tactical principles you will lose your cache. As in urban areas, I believe the cache will be approached and dug up immediately once the observers think you are out of the area.

You will always find great places to cache; the hard part will be picking good places you can cache without being seen. This is much harder in urban areas, of course. Caching requires a smart, tactical mind, especially in a survival situation where people will be looking at and salvaging anything they think can be of use for their survival or barter material. Periodically, check on your caches while hunting, wood or water gathering, or security patrolling. There is no need to approach the cache site any closer than you need to make sure the site has not been found. Good tactical principles and a little luck will ensure your caches stay safe from prying eyes and others who would look on stealing a cache as good luck in their survival efforts. When burying weapons and ammunition, beware of metal detectors. Do a double cache—dig a deep hole for your weapons or ammunition and have at least a foot or more of dirt, then have a cache of tools or nails, bolts, etc. Hopefully anyone using a metal detector will not check further after finding the tools. In tests this has been the case every time.

When preparing, a little practice caching will go a long way in making you successful if disaster strikes. I am not saying that bad luck will not get your caches found—that is always a possibility. Caching, as is everything else in a survival environment, is not a guarantee you will be successful. There is always an enhanced chance of success if the tactical techniques discussed previously are followed. But remember, your group is most likely not the only trained group out there, and everyone is in a survival situation, which makes everything fair, including the finding and taking of someone else's cache site. You must become an expert at restoring the area to its natural look. This is easier said than done.

When choosing rural cache sites, pick areas that would not lend themselves to development—not that you would have this worry after the disaster—such as steep hills, cliff areas, scree slopes, etc. Before the disaster, caching in an area where you plan to leave the cache until needed may be a problem if a developer builds a housing area over your cache. I have heard stories of this actually happening to people before. With GPSs available, always have a GPS coordinate of the site. Stay away from power lines and outstanding or known natural sites, as many folks use these places to look for things buried with metal detectors. The more remote the area, the better. At the end of the day, there is always a chance that either man will find it or nature will take it away. There are no guarantees. As with anything, good planning, research, and proper technique lend themselves to success.

Chapter Ten

References

My intent is to provide some references for survival-oriented equipment and information. In no way am I endorsing any products. You will have to make your own decisions. My personal belief is if you are just starting out to prepare, you are behind the power curve. I do not know how far. Hopefully, there is still time, so make good use of it.

All references here were taken from publicly accessible documents on the Internet.

Survival Magazines

Survivalist	survivalist.com
Real World Survivor	realworldsurvivor.com
Backwoodsman	backwoodsmanmag.com
Backwoods Home	backwoodshome.com
Backpacker	backpacker.com
Outdoor Survival	outdoorsurvivalmagazine.com

There are certainly more survival magazines available; these were found on a web search. There are also survival books that have been written by various survival experts, and a web search will find these quickly. All are full of worthwhile survival information.

Survival Books

The Complete Survival Guide edited by Mark Thiffault
SAS Survival Handbook by John "Lofty" Wiseman
Extreme Survival by Marshall Corwin

Tactical Training

Whether it is weapons training, martial arts, land navigation, or medical, all training and the schools and individuals that do it are on the Internet. Search the equipment or training protocol you are interested in, and it will appear on your screen. We all are fortunate to have this capability, and hopefully it will be around for as long as anyone needs it, but there are no guarantees. I have no dog in this fight; I stick with my advice in this book, which is get to work, look for experienced people near you, and see if they are interested in starting a group. Until that happens, start using the lists in this book, and start your individual preparations.

Guns and Ammunition

American Derringer	amderringer.com/guns.html
Armalite	armalite.com
Auto Ordnance	auto-ordnance.com
Barrett	barrett.net
Beretta	berettausa.com/default.aspx
Benelli	benelliusa.com
Blaser	blaser-usa.com
Bond Arms	bondarms.com
Browning	browning.com
Bushmaster	bushmaster.com/index.asp
Century Arms	centuryarms.com

Charter Arms	charterfirearms.com/index.html
Colt	coltsmfg.com/Default.aspx
Crosman	crosman.com/airguns
CZ	cz-usa.com
Daisy	daisy.com
DPMS Panther Arms	dpmsinc.com
European American Arms	eaacorp.com
Fausti Shotguns	faustiusa.com
Franchi	franchiusa.com
Freedom Arms	freedomarms.com
Glock	glock.com
Harrington & Richardson	hr1871.com/default.asp
Henry Rifles	henryrepeating.com/henry-rifles.cfm
Kahr Arms	kahr.com
Kel-Tec	keltecweapons.com
Kimber	kimberamerica.com
Legacy Sports	legacysports.com
Les Baer	lesbaer.com
Magnum Research	magnumresearch.com
Marlin	marlinfirearms.com
Mossberg	mossberg.com
North American Arms	naaminis.com
Olympic Arms	olyarms.com
Para-Ordnance	paraord.com
Remington	remington.com
Rock River Arms	rockriverarms.com
Rossi	rossiusa.com
Ruger	ruger.com/index.html
Savage Arms	savagearms.com
Sig Sauer	sigsauer.com/Default.aspx

Smith & Wesson	smith-wesson.com
Springfield Armory	springfield-armory.com
Steyr Arms	steyrarms.com
Stoeger	stoegerindustries.com
Thompson Center	tcarms.com
Taurus	taurususa.com
Tristar Sporting Arms	tristarsportingarms.com
Uberti	uberti.com
Wilson Combat	wilsoncombat.com
Winchester	winchesterguns.com

Many gun manufacturers also make ammunition. I am sure with a more detailed search of the Internet that more manufacturers could be found. Start your preparation with the guns you currently own. If you have the weapons recommended in this book, good. If you have others, you still have the means of self-defense.

Rather than have this chapter be hundreds of pages long, I will put the equipment name and then a suggested term to type into your computer. All suggestions were tried by me personally and were satisfactory for my quest for information.

Tactical Equipment

There are many tactical equipment manufacturers, and you will have to make your own choices. Tactical equipment, such as harnesses, vests, belts, and other equipment carriers, is the difference between carrying your equipment comfortably and organized to where you can get to needed gear quickly when situations require it or fumbling around for it while someone kills you. Once you start acquiring the equipment, practice with it in training. You should be able to access any gear on your body in the dark or under duress. A well-trained group will have the same equipment in the same place on their gear so if a member is injured, others could find it in the dark. Also, where singular pieces of critical equipment are being carried by a single group member should be known by all. This is good tactical planning that leaves nothing to chance.

Water Purification

There are several survival straws and items of survival purification equipment that come up. Remember that polluted water will kill you as surely as any weapon. Do not take a chance on any water found after disaster—purify it by boiling or filtering. Many purification systems can be found using your search engine. Purifying water will be an absolute necessity for survival.

steripen.com – potableaqua.com – buylifestraw.com – katadyn.com – renovowater.com – arcticfilters.com

Commercial Water Distillers

These small water distillers only require heat from a stove or fire to turn dirty water into steam and back into drinkable water. They are a great survival tool to ensure the group is drinking safe water.

waterwise.com – survivalstill.com

Survival Food Sources

Survival food websites such as WiseFoodStorage.com, BuyEmergencyFoods.com, PrepareWise.com, and foodinsurance.com do not cover what can be bought in grocery stores, such as beans, rice, buckwheat, etc. All have a use and will provide you with packaged and secure food that has a long shelf life, which will be needed for any long-term survival. Spoiled or bad food can be just as deadly or incapacitating as bad water. You cannot afford to become so debilitated that you cannot function nor do what has to be done in an emergency. Check all food before eating, and purify all water before drinking.

Fire Starting Sources

There are several commercial fire starters on the market. I am an old guy who has started fires in some terrible conditions with just matches and the wood I could find. Some was cut from downed logs and standing dead trees. It took time, and I suspect in any cold, rain, or snow situation it will be hard to find dry wood or tinder. There are some fire starters worth looking at.

Lightning-strike fire starter – hollandguns.com

The blast match fire starter is another commercial starter. Type in blast match in your search engine.

Survival Fast Fire Kit – solkoasurvival.com

There are many other fire starters that can be found with a simple search on your computer. One of my standby favorites is homemade of melted wax, wood chips, and fire starter fluid hardened into small blocks. It works every time a flame is put to it. But do not get me wrong, starting a fire in the dark while it's raining will not be something to look forward to.

Field Stoves

Anyone with a little knowledge can make a camp or hobo stove. Small fire pits are also used to cook food and heat water. I am putting a couple of commercial field stoves in here because they concentrate the heat for quicker cooking with less wood. There are many others out there, and sporting goods or camping stores have a large variety. I am listing a couple here that work with wood, are small, and are easily used. I think a quick look at the following websites will give you an idea of several choices that are available.

solostove.com – firebox.com

Groups who have a plan to move to a rural location should include at least two good wood-burning cooking stoves in their survival location. They should also have extra parts, such as glass, handles, and any other parts that may need replacing over time. A trip to a wood stove store would get any questions you have answered. Keep in mind, if you live in an area with harsh winters, basic survival will be decided by your ability to heat your location. Also keep in mind that the heating of your location with fire will give your location away by sight and smell to anyone in the area.

Tie-Down Straps

You will need several different tie-down straps, come-a-longs, and tow straps to assist your move to a rural site, to secure equipment in your survival site, or to barricade your survival site. I will list a couple of websites here to help your search. Tie-downs and tow straps are

Keep in mind that the heating of your location with fire could give your location away. (zlikovec, courtesy of iStock)

easily found at retail stores. Like most special need items, when you need them and do not have them, almost nothing else will do. titanstraps.com – americanriggingsupply.com

Flashlights

Having the ability to see at night will be mandatory. You will never have enough batteries and will eventually run out, but to start you need a good, durable, tactical-grade flashlight. The following websites are suggestions to start your search, but there are many others easily found. The decisions must be yours. I have also verified over the years that you can never have enough flashlights, so get more than one per group member. surefire.com – 511tactical.com – nitecore.com – streamlight.com

Night Vision

I believe night vision is critical to success in night operations, and that will not change in a survival situation. If a group can afford them, I highly recommend having them. They have saved my life several times in my past careers. If looters or raiders have them and the people they are attacking do not, there is a good chance the looters will win. There are many night vision and thermal devices available. Like any other piece of equipment, they must be trained on and maintained by the user. I also know if time runs out and disaster strikes, only a miniscule part of the nation's population will have night vision devices in their possession.

tnvc.com – opticsplanet.com – nvdepot.com

Medical Kits

If serious injuries occur after disaster strikes, you are in trouble. Using my own experience, I am trained to give first aid for trauma wounds. I can stop the bleeding, ensure airways are open, and treat or prevent shock, and I have done this several times on the battlefield. However, I can tell you if a close family member is shot in the head, chest, or stomach, if I cannot call 911 or get him or her to a hospital, he or she is going to die. I cannot perform surgery without a 95 percent chance that I would be the one who caused his or her death. By all means, you should get medical training and have a good kit available, but unless you are a surgeon with the right tools, you are going to watch seriously injured group members die. There is no discussion for individual survivors—if you get shot in a vital area, you will die.

promedkits.com – adventuremedicalkits.com – first-aid-product. com – survival-supply.com

This chapter is to get you started. You will never have enough equipment to live your life like you did before disaster strikes. I believe the quicker you accept this and adapt to your new situation, the better you will do. As time goes by after the disaster and you continue to survive, all the materials in your area will become available to you as people die or leave. This guarantees nothing other than if the group is smart and takes the initiative, you can make your life more secure or comfortable with the equipment you acquire. However, you will still have to do everything within a tactical and survival situation. We currently live in a world that is fairly secure, but should disaster strike, everything we need to have a comfortable life will be taken away from us.

Chapter Eleven

Life After

I have been asked to give an example of life after the disaster as I see it. I will try to present it as I envision the unending Survive While Surviving lifestyle that will be forced upon us.

Thirty Days After Disaster

Mary was at her security position at the back bedroom window of the group's survival location. She, along with the other three members, had been on since two in the morning. It was now around six and starting to get light. She was a little hungry but not really bad. The group leaders had started serious rationing of the group's store of food once the lights went out and did not come back on. There had been riots downtown, and she could see the smoke rising from several fires. She looked around the room at the piles of equipment the group had been smart enough to acquire before the disaster and the sleeping forms of other group members laying among the equipment. She was looking forward to a few hours of sleep once she was relieved by the day crew.

She looked out over the yard and into the field of grass that was an empty lot behind the group's survival location. Nothing was moving yet. They had been fairly lucky—so far there had been several groups of people—probably potential looters the group leaders had warned about—but all had vacated the area once they were challenged by armed group members. On one occasion a week ago, two men actually got close to the house and were shot by the day crew when they raised their weapons. Both were killed and their bodies stripped of weapons, ammunition, packs, and clothes. Their bodies had been buried in the center of the vacant lot in shallow graves.

The only other thing of consequence was a gang of around twenty men and women, some armed with rifles, seen walking two blocks from the house, but they were going toward town and were not seen again. It was now light enough to see several blocks away, and she knew the day crew would be relieving her soon. As she was glancing out over the vacant field, a slight movement caught her attention. She looked at the area but could see nothing else. She thought it might have been a small rodent or rabbit. She lifted her rifle and looked through the nine-power scope directly at the location of the movement. She jumped in surprise when a rifle barrel and a gloved hand appeared to be laying in the grass. As she looked closer through the scope, she realized she was looking at a well-camouflaged person crawling toward the house.

Without looking she kicked the closest sleeping group member, who awoke with a start. She whispered, "Get everyone up quietly, we have people moving on us. Get everyone into their defensive positions." As group members were awakened and moved into their positions, she looked back through the scope. She could now see that the individual was closer. She also knew she would not be able to see him with her naked eye unless she knew exactly where to look—this individual was the point of coming trouble. She sighted in on what she determined to be the head and took a well-aimed shot. She was surprised by the spray of blood and the sight of the target rolling sideways and then laying still. His rifle was now completely exposed. Almost immediately, several bullets hit the side of the house and ricocheted loudly off the brick walls. One or two bullets came through the firing port in the window and missed Mary by inches. Then it all became quiet.

Ben, one of the group leaders, slid up beside her and looked around the edge of the firing port. Mary explained what she had seen, and the inert body spoke for itself. Ben turned and said, "Good job, kid. Had you not been on this, we would have had some real close-range problems. We still need to see what we have here." As if on signal, two more rounds came through the firing port and missed Ben by inches. Ben said, "They are good shots and most likely using scoped rifles. Everyone needs to stay out of sight and observe from cover." Two shots rang out from the front room of the structure, and a group member said, "One down!" In the front yard, three others were moving away. Ben felt like he was back in the Army and Iraq all over again.

An hour later, no further movement had been seen, and no shots had been fired. While half the group ate their morning rations, half the group watched. All were glad the group had cleared the imme-diate surrounding areas of brush and cover. Ben looked around at the group. Everyone had their gear on per group practices, and their weapons were ready. Ben knew the group of thirty-four was in good shape with food, water, and ammunition stores on hand. He made a quick decision that no gathering party was going out today until they determined what they were up against. One of the things the group had done after assembling was cutting three holes in the walls at ceiling level on the second floor. Group members were now looking through these with binoculars and were positive that whoever had attacked them had withdrawn from the area.

It was determined that a three-man security group would exit the back of the building and patrol out to the end of the survival site's observation or three hundred yards, whichever came first, while covered by the survival site. The three group members, following instructions, broke cover once outside, ran ten meters, and dropped into prone position. No shots were fired at them, and the second-story observers reported no sightings of movement or people. An hour later, the patrol was back. There had been no sightings. A detail was sent out to strip the two bodies and bury them in the field. A group meeting was then held, and all were in attendance except the eight guards—two on each side of the survival site with four downstairs and four on the second floor—all with scoped rifles or binoculars. The meeting opened with good news; Mary was congratulated for her good work, and it was reported that two very good scoped rifles, three combat pistols, and other gear was taken from the two bodies.

The bad news was that they had been found by a well-trained and equipped group. How large the group was was not known, so it was decided the extra four guards would stay on each shift throughout the night and everyone would sleep with their fighting gear on. If no action was taken against them, a gathering and recon patrol party would depart at first light. The party would be covered by the survival location until out of sight. The group leaders knew they had gotten away lucky that morning, but bad things were coming the group's way. If nothing else, whoever tried them this morning would want revenge for the two of their group that were lost. The gathering and recon party was picked, and they immediately started planning the move out of the survival site and the route they would take on their mission. Everyone knew the upgraded actions that were now in place would become a daily way of life for the group. Because of the unknown tactical situation, the gathering and recon party would not use any of the group's vehicles. They would move on foot with designated group members as a reaction force if they made contact. The group would not use their vehicles unless absolutely necessary, as available fuel was, as far as the group knew, nonexistent in the local area.

This short story is certainly close to what will happen in the event of a real disaster. The group was well trained and weathered the event, but had they not been trained or had they been a single family, they most likely would not have survived the morning. The sad thing here is that the untrained among us are the majority of the population. Should disaster strike, many will quickly find themselves in dire danger that they may not be able to fend off.

If you look at this short scenario from a tactical standpoint, you can come to a lot of conclusions. One would be that the group did well because Mary was awake and doing her job. Had she fallen asleep or not been focused on the job at hand, the group would have at least taken some casualties from a close-range attack. At worst it could have either been run out of its well-stocked survival location or been wiped out. In critical situations, it is often the little things that keep you alive. Mary taking a short nap at a critical time could have been a disaster the group may not have survived.

A second conclusion could have been different than depicted in this scenario. The three-man security patrol could have been ambushed and one or all of them killed. The group then would have found themselves in a standoff with an unknown number of attackers. Also, the burying party that went out could have been attacked by a returning attack group. Ben and his group would then be faced with several possibilities from going out to save the burying party to losing them and being in a standoff situation with the attackers. The following morning, the gathering and recon patrol party could have been ambushed and sustained many casualties, which would have immediately affected Ben's group and forced some serious decisions or actions.

Another scenario could have been that the attacking group was large and had the capability to put the survival site under siege. The group in the survival site would have some serious decisions regarding whether could they break the siege. Would accurate fire on the attackers break the siege? Would the group have to raid outside the site to break the siege? A multitude of possibilities would end in the group's success or demise.

I mention these possibilities to get you thinking about how fragile your existence may be in a survival situation and how quickly your situation can change for the worse. Even doing everything correctly does not mean that unplanned situations will not plague you and threaten the group's survival. The ability to adapt and react to unplanned events is critical and is always done better by prepared and trained disciplined groups. There is no news here for experienced professionals but mandatory reading and understanding by everyone else. Your survival under severe circumstances stands in the balance.

Chapter Twelve

Final Thoughts

Hopefully, this book will be read by people who will never need it. Being prepared is just good common sense, but having to live in a survival and tactical situation is a backbreaking, mind-numbing lifestyle that I do not wish on anyone. The truth is, I believe that it is a possibility based on ongoing world events, but hopefully I am wrong. Whatever event kicks off a national disaster—a power grid failure, national anarchy, or a natural disaster with national implications—really makes no difference. If it goes long term, as discussed in this book, the results will be the same. With my career experience, I cannot fully determine what will happen if the population's vital services are suddenly cut off. I do know that in our large population centers, it will turn violent quickly, and people will have to be prepared to defend themselves and the goods they possess. To see how quickly things can go bad, just look at Ferguson, Baltimore, and the Rodney King riots.

As this book is being written, the news is full of reports that do not look good for the future. Some recent reports include:

- If the national power grid is disrupted for a year, possibly 90 percent of the population may perish.
- Homeland security and FEMA are unprepared for a nuclear attack or major natural disaster.
- Major terrorist attacks should be expected.
- Civil unrest on a national scale is possible.
- An EMP attack could be launched from any of several countries, which would knock out all power-generating capabilities nationwide.
- The national and international financial systems may collapse.

This is a short list of what is being reported. If you put it together with weak or nonexistent leadership from our nation's capital, at least some of what we have talked about in this book is possible—most likely with no warning. With that being said, I want readers of this book to ask themselves some questions.

- How prepared are you if you had to survive for three months starting right now?
- If five looters came onto your property and started forcing their way into your house, do you have the means to stop them?
- What emergency family plans have you made and rehearsed?
- If major rioting broke out, forcing you from your home, where are you going and how are you going to get there?
- If you have family members on life support requiring electricity, what is the plan for them if power is interrupted indefinitely?

If your answers to these questions are "I do not know," there is a good chance you will be part of the predicted 90 percent who do not make it. You hear all the time that it will happen sooner rather than later, that could be within the hour, or within the time you have left to live. It comes down to responsibility. It is your duty to prepare to protect your family or the people who depend on you. If you're alone, it's your responsibility to care for yourself and anybody around you that needs help. It's been that way throughout history, and many have stepped up and taken that responsibility, but many have waited until too late. What are your thoughts? If you read this book, you know mine.

I believe some areas will maintain some form of society and control of the situation. If you are in an area where this happens, the support of the effort to maintain order is paramount and a benefit to all. Everyone needs to pull together to make it work. These areas should also be on their guard for looters or raiders from outside the area. It's a given that if large areas of the country are in crisis mode, sooner or later it will bleed over into the areas that are not. It is also a given that groups of looters and raiders may be large in numbers and well armed.

With total long-term disaster not previously happening in our country, there is no actual history of what would really take place over the long term, but a good case can be made by looking at some of the short-term disasters, such as Katrina. We all know what went on in New Orleans in the week after the storm. What if no federal or state help was available? I believe the looting, survival actions of starving people and those trapped by high waters, would be enhanced many times over and would force the moves and actions discussed in this book by both security forces and the general populace.

Looking at what is going on with the demonstrations against police in many of our major cities, it is not hard to feel that anarchy is only a step away. Should major rioting break out, all survival and defense situations will start to impact millions of people in our big cities— even if it only lasted a few days. If you and your family were caught up in it, do you have the means to survive the incident? If you want to fully understand what happens when there is no security force to put a stop to it when a population is unprepared and not equipped to take care of itself, you only have to turn on the news to see what ISIS is doing to the Yazidi tribe and other people in the areas it has captured. I made reference in this book to what happens when an armed violent group attacks an unarmed group, and the result historically is that the unarmed and unprepared group ceases to exist or is used as the armed group sees fit.

A while back I had a conversation with a young man who is preparing, and his idea was to have some cows, goats, and pigs on his survival site. He is in a rural area and can certainly entertain that thought and get the animals, and in the preparation phase this will work. Once disaster strikes and a long-term situation exists, anyone with animals will have to change the way they do business. The first question once feed stores are no longer operating is going to be to feed them. Once disaster strikes, any animals will be targeted as a food source and will have to be guarded, which is another job requiring full-time people. In this situation, animals cannot be allowed to graze free range, as they will not be around long in that situation. Having any animals will put additional guard and maintenance requirements on the group. It is a good idea to have them, but it also puts a heavy workload on the group. That workload may include building a secure area to keep them in, the planting and growing of feed, and a larger group or the chance of losing the animals and all they provide.

Winters in some of our states, including where I live, produce subzero weather with high winds, which brings the chill factor down as low as thirty to fifty below zero. I have been asked how you manage to survive during this type of weather. An easy answer is that you don't if away from support or home, and many people in these areas who make mistakes in travel planning or breakdowns do not. In normal times, with heating and utilities available, it's fairly easy; just pay your bills and plan. In a survival situation, you will find yourself in a triple-threat situation of surviving, Surviving While Surviving, and maintaining a warm shelter out of the wind with a full-time fire. This situation puts an added logistical responsibility of procuring firewood on you. If firewood is scarce and the area you are in has harsh winters, a move to a new location may be forced. Planning and awareness should prevent this from catching the group by surprise. The impact on Surviving While Surviving or the tactical situation is that everyone will be confined to dealing with the same conditions. Other groups will be looking to loot firewood, thus adding to everyone's guard and tactical requirements.

When living in an area where winters are harsh, all winter clothing and bedding must be stored and maintained during the summer months. Should the group be run out of the survival site by circumstances, the winter gear must leave with them or they are on borrowed time. The maintaining of gear required for survival during harsh weather conditions is another primary planning point that cannot be ignored. There is a tendency during summer weather to forget about winter gear, but this cannot be done in a survival situation. As the people who live in remote areas of Alaska or some of our mountain states know, preparation for the next winter starts when the current one is over.

One of the things I wonder about is what government support can be counted on if disaster strikes. I have been told a few times in discussions that if a national disaster strikes, people will, for a time, have to do what they must to survive. My question is what does that mean? Does it mean it is okay to become a looter or raider? Is it okay to take someone else's food and water by force—maybe hurting or killing them in doing so? To this question, I cannot get a straight answer. I suspect it means we're in it alone, and if or when things stabilize, politicians will be looking to press charges against individuals who did what they did to survive. There are, again, no good answers here. In my mind, self-defense is self-defense if you are the one being attacked. I guess under current thoughts of the leaders I've talked to, if you are looting, you are doing what you have to in the survival situation you are in.

There are a lot of good, organized people in every community, and if these individuals are trying to restore some semblance of order, it should not be lost on individuals and groups that aligning themselves with these efforts will benefit all concerned. Should disaster strike on a national or world order, nothing will be simple again. The more orderly and independent communities in smaller population areas can become, the more they may be the best places to be, as they will be able to get the work done that will ensure survival and community protection. This does not mean acquiring food and water will be easier, but with an organized community-sized group taking part in hunting, fishing, and gardening, the chance of success is raised considerably.

It should not be lost on anybody that the more people you can bring together with talent and knowledge, the more you will have available to ensure the success of the effort. In the past, there have been groups that could have been successful in their endeavors but were destroyed by infighting and disorganization. I have only one recommendation here, and that is leaders must not let this happen and must guard against it. In saying that, it ultimately will be up to the community should disaster strike. Like most things in this book, I can give advice but in the end will have no control over anyone other than the group I am with. If luck or situation goes against me, I may not have control over what happens to my group or myself.

You will always need more equipment than you have—that is a given. If you have the people or transportation to carry it, there are no issues, but if you do not, all decisions you make in what you keep or discard will be life or death decisions. Unfortunately, the ability to make some decisions comes from experience. In this situation, I can only wish you luck in making the right ones. I do not intend for this book to make you think all is lost. There is always hope, and any training or preparation you do before the disaster will go a long way toward your hopes coming true, but there are no guarantees.

This book cannot guarantee your success; neither can any experts guarantee your success should disaster strike. You and your group, if you have one, will be at the mercy of good or bad luck and fate. Prior preparation and training will increase your ability to survive but will not guarantee it. It is a given that most untrained people are looking for perfect answers when training or reading new material, but I can safely tell you that there are none. Go into everything with an open mind, learn what you can, and acquire what you can to assist your efforts, but count on nothing going the way you may want it to be.

Should there be a long-term disaster, each group and individual will initially make decisions based on what is in their best interests. Countries do that now. I have no issues with that, as I will be doing the same thing, but I caution everyone to keep an open mind. If there are local governments still working, check them out. It may be in the group's best interest to join them, but it may also be in the group's best interest to move out of the area. Those decisions will probably be life or death decisions. The main thing to look for is that everyone is being treated equally and fairly; there should be no second-class citizens.

With the information contained in this book, you have enough information to start your preparation. The individuals and groups out there that are and have been preparing for disaster already know about the information I have put in this chapter and, most likely, in this book. If I have put anything in this book that those preparing said upon reading, "I didn't think of that," then this book is a double success. Hopefully this information convinces those not preparing to start and assists those that are preparing to be more effective in what they are doing. We all may be going into a situation where we will have to Survive While Surviving. Good luck to both groups in all you do.

The comments and suggestions in this book are my own and are based on a fifty-three-year career in the tactical and security fields. I have been to many countries where, due to politics, certain groups and tribal hatreds cause people to live a survival lifestyle. I know what it looks like. I also know my own country's history and the violence that lives just below the surface of our civilization. Should disaster strike on a national level, in most areas of this country we will certainly step back hundreds, if not thousands, of years. With a population that has mostly had everything available to them, I cannot see anything but what has been depicted in this book. I hope I am wrong, but only history will be the judge of that.

Steve Mattoon
2016

Glossary

Ambush

A surprise attack against an unsuspecting enemy or group, usually from a prepared position.

Booby Trap

A device that injures someone who is doing a normal act.

Caching

The art of hiding material and equipment in any environment.

Combat Harness

A commercially made vest or harness to carry tactical gear.

Combat Pistol

Usually an automatic pistol with a seven- to fifteen-round magazine.

Combat Shotgun

Short-barreled shotgun with combat sights, such as the police Remington 870.

Dump Bag
A pouch on your gear where expended magazines are placed for future use.

EMP
Electromagnetic pulse, can be either natural (solar flare) or man-made (nuclear) and could knock out all electrical circuits, including vehicles.

FEMA
Federal Emergency Management Agency

Gathering Party
Part of the survival group responsible for finding what the group needs to survive.

Hunting Shotgun
Long-barreled shotgun used for geese and duck hunting, can be used with the right ammunition for deer and other game.

M4
Short combat version of the M16/AR15 rifle series.

MREs
Meals Ready to Eat, commercially packaged combat rations for the military that are also available to civilians.

Raid
A planned attack on a location with the intent of destroying it, occupying it, or taking what material is needed from the site.

Rally Point
A planned location the group members go if they get separated.

Running Password
A preselected word the whole group knows that members will use for identification if running into the rally point after dark.

Semiauto
Guns that fire one round every time you pull the trigger.

SOP

Standard Operating Procedures, how the group performs regular or routine actions.

Survival Location

A fixed site or structure intended for survival and defense.

Tactical Movement

Secure formations used by the group when moving or fighting.

Index